# Overtourism

# Overtourism

*The Role of Effective Destination Management*

Helene von Magius Møgelhøj

**BEP**

BUSINESS EXPERT PRESS

*Leader in applied, concise business books*

*Overtourism: The Role of Effective Destination Management*

Copyright © Business Expert Press, LLC, 2021.

Cover design by Charlene Kronstedt

Interior design by Exeter Premedia Services Private Ltd., Chennai, India

First published in 2021 by
Business Expert Press, LLC
222 East 46th Street, New York, NY 10017
www.businessexpertpress.com

ISBN-13: 978-1-63742-060-7 (paperback)
ISBN-13: 978-1-63742-061-4 (e-book)

Business Expert Press Tourism and Hospitality Management Collection

Collection ISSN: 2375-9623 (print)
Collection ISSN: 2375-9631 (electronic)

First edition: 2021

10 9 8 7 6 5 4 3 2 1

# Description

*Overtourism* examines the increasingly important role of destination management and effective stakeholder engagement in order to maximize the economic contribution of tourism while avoiding the potential pitfalls of overtourism.

Rapid growth in international tourism has led to the emergence of the overtourism phenomenon. It is a situation where large tourist numbers start to cause tensions with local residents and communities owing to what they consider to be negative impacts on their quality of life including overcrowding, congestion, housing shortages, and changes in the retail sector. Overtourism can occur in any type of destination be it urban or rural in a developed or developing country.

The author does not consider a global reduction in international travel as a likely long-term solution to addressing overtourism. Rather destinations should prepare for continuous growth in both international tourist arrivals and domestic tourism in the longer term. Overtourism can often be reversed or averted through effective destination management. This requires engaging with key stakeholders and the local community to ensure that the local residents' quality of life is preserved while at the same time delivering a high-quality experience for visitors. The coronavirus pandemic has provided destinations with an opportunity to reflect and decide how they want to recover to become more resilient and sustainable in the long term.

# Keywords

overtourism; tourism; mass tourism; destination management; destination management organization; DMO; stakeholder engagement; stakeholder management; sustainability; carrying capacity; climate change; congestion; day-trippers; Airbnb; sharing economy; staycation; digitalization; social media; quality of life; local host community; local residents; planning; visitor infrastructure; seasonality; dispersion; diversification; tourism product development; tourism-related infrastructure; responsible tourism; recovery; resilience; COVID-19; adaptation; visitor flow management; performance measurement; global mass mobility; localism; authenticity; social inclusivity; sustainable development goals; strategic alignment; investment; funding; taxation

# Contents

# Introduction and Overview

## Purpose and Plan of the Book

The idea for this book was conceived before the coronavirus pandemic took hold in March 2020. At the end of 2019, overtourism was a frequently discussed topic in the media and among tourism professionals across the globe. The conversation's focus was on how do we manage the exponential growth in tourism at destination level to avoid being overwhelmed by overtourism. No one knew that by mid-2020 tourism would come to a virtual standstill causing much concern and exposing the economic fragility in tourism-dependent destinations. However, this book does not consider a global reduction in international travel as a likely long-term solution to addressing overtourism. Rather destinations should prepare for continuous growth in both international tourist arrivals and domestic tourism in the longer term.

For now, mass tourism and in turn overtourism have been paused, but it seems inevitable that these will return in the future if destinations do not take prompt action before the growth in international tourism resumes. In the short term, social distancing measures mean that those destinations most exposed to overtourism will have to be managed better. This puts pressure on destination management organizations (DMOs) to pause and reflect on the type of tourism and visitors they wish to attract going forward. DMOs will need to engage with the destination's key industry stakeholders and local host population to ensure that maximum benefit is delivered at the destination level be that economically, socio-culturally, or environmentally. The power and influence of key individual stakeholders, such as airport and port authorities, are often overlooked at the destination level. This can result in failure to accept and implement strategies and actions designed to address overtourism and ensure long-term sustainability of the tourism industry.

This book seeks to examine and analyze the causes of overtourism and how this negative phenomenon, and consequence of the exponential growth in international travel and tourism, can be managed or even reversed through effective destination management. Essentially, this requires strong stakeholder collaboration and engagement with the local community at the destination level combined with an appropriate DMO structure. Too often the main role of DMOs is merely marketing and promotion rather than managing visitors once they have arrived at the destination. For many DMOs the primary objective is to attract more visitors and to ensure maximum utilization of the tourism-related infrastructure such as hotels and visitor attractions rather than managing visitors. One of the critical success factors for destinations is to better understand the value of the different types of visitors they attract. This knowledge allows destinations to focus on those segments that provide the most benefits at the local level and tends to be overnight staying visitors rather than daytrippers.

If anything, the coronavirus pandemic has exposed the dire consequences for destinations that are too dependent on tourism, and the accompanying economic fragility this can cause. The crisis has highlighted the importance of having a balanced economy rather than relying on tourism as the main industry sector. Tourism as part of an equitable economy should probably equate to less than 10 percent of gross domestic product (GDP)/gross value added (GVA) being derived from the tourism in a country or destination.

It is important to bear in mind that there are many benefits associated with a successful tourism industry. The sector plays an important role in promoting the attractiveness and appeal of a place not only as a destination to visit but also as a place to live, work, study, and invest. Tourism supports the preservation and conservation of cultural and natural heritage assets. At the same time, the many micro-, small-, and medium-sized enterprises (SMEs) operating in the tourism sector are responsible for creating vital local jobs and contributing to economic growth and prosperity. However, in order to be successful, destinations need to be managed effectively with a focus on sustainability, people, planet, and profit.

## Limitations of Scope

This book seeks to illustrate the positive steps that destinations and DMOs can take to develop and manage their tourism sector in a more sustainable manner that brings benefits and economic prosperity to the local host population while avoiding overtourism and some of the associated negative social and environmental impacts.

The book acknowledges that travel and tourism is set to continue to grow as an aspirational activity in the long term. Although, the exponential growth in travel was paused momentarily by the coronavirus pandemic, it is recognized that people always have and will travel when they are able to do so.

Therefore, destinations and DMOs should consider how they can work smarter and introduce measures to better manage visitor flows as well as seeking to attract those visitors who deliver the most added value at the local level. This in turn should help guarantee that a destination's carrying capacity is managed rather than exceeded and situations that give rise to tourism phobia and antitourism campaigns are avoided. Achieving effective destination management requires a systematic approach to measuring and monitoring a destination's performance according to a set of agreed key indicators. Furthermore, destinations should pursue a flexible long-term strategy supported by an appropriate action and implementation plan with short-, medium-, and long-term goals.

As the travel and tourism industry is highly fragmented there are no easy solutions, nor a one-size-fits-all model that will work for every single destination. However, there are numerous common issues which means that destinations can learn from each other without compromising their individual uniqueness and in turn competitive advantage. Thus, this book looks at destination management examples that can make DMOs more effective in overcoming the overtourism challenge by introducing measures to monitor, manage, and disperse visitor flows in order to avoid saturation. Part of the solution is to effectively engage with the local host population and key industry stakeholders in a collaborative manner in order to achieve strategic alignment. In general, this requires a multidisciplinary crosscutting approach to destination management that addresses tourism in a holistic manner. Tourism needs to be fully integrated into the destination's wider regulatory and policy framework and not considered in isolation.

This book aims to highlight how destinations can avoid falling victim to overtourism. By adopting an effective destination management model, destinations can benefit from a successful tourism industry in the long run. An effective destination management model requires measuring and monitoring trends on an ongoing basis in order to anticipate and plan for the future.

# CHAPTER 1

# Introduction to Overtourism

## Introduction

Until the advent of the coronavirus pandemic in 2020, the rapid growth in international tourism over the past few decades led to the emergence of the overtourism phenomenon. The term *overtourism* officially entered the Oxford English Dictionary in 2018 as one of its words of the year. It is defined as:

> an excessive number of visitors heading to famous locations, damaging the environment and having a detrimental impact on residents' lives.

It is a situation where large tourist numbers start to cause tensions with the local residents and communities due to what they consider to be negative impacts on their quality of life including overcrowding, congestion, housing shortages, and changes in the retail sector. Overtourism is not necessarily about too many visitors overall, but rather too many visitors in a specific location at a certain time. This is particularly true from the local host population's perspective in terms of their perception of overcrowdedness and a reduced quality of life. Overtourism is generally associated with the volume of visitors, visitor characteristics, time of visit, and the destination's carrying capacity. It is rarely caused by a single issue but is instead caused by a combination of factors. These in turn cause a wide range of problems including environmental degradation, litter, congestion, and pollution.

Overtourism can occur in any type of destination, be it urban or rural in a developed or developing country. However, it tends to occur more frequently in mature urban areas rather than emerging rural destinations. Between 75 and 80 percent of all tourism takes place in cities according to the United Nations World Tourism Organization (UNWTO)

(UNWTO Webinar "Agenda 2030 and SDGs in times of COVID-19: the chance to true recovery"—Tourism for SDGs 2020). Cities tend have good access by air, rail, road, and/or sea. Furthermore, they usually offer a wide range of easily accessible attractions. Overtourism occurs when the ratio between tourists and locals reaches a pinch point and the destination becomes saturated. Basically, the destination becomes too popular for its own good or a victim of its own success. The negative impacts of overtourism may in turn lead to the destination going into decline as the quality of the visitor experience deteriorates.

## Overtourism Definitions

Dr. Claudio Milano describes "overtourism as a complex journey between economic gain, sociocultural preservation and responsible futures" (Milano 2017). Essentially, overtourism results from a combination of a rapid evolution in visitor numbers based on unsustainable destination management practices and policies as well as greed among individuals and organizations benefitting financially from increased visitor volumes. This in turn creates "tourism phobia" in local communities who consider that "their" urban spaces have been compromised by visitors and the related infrastructure and services, diminishing the overall quality of life and causing anxiety. The root causes of this "tourism phobia" include the lost sense of belonging, decreasing local people's purchasing power, and unaffordable real estate, which can result in an antagonistic divide between hosts and visitors. He considers overtourism to be a direct result of the growing evolution of unsustainable mass tourism practices.

According to Richard Crasta:

> Global mass tourism was and is often hailed and justified by those for whom it is a money-spinner, foreign exchange earner, an engine of livelihood, or a raison d'être: hotel owners, travel industry workers, and operators of tourist attractions, government tourism departments whose existence and expansion depends on the number of tourists arrivals, capitalists who own the resources, the prime real estate (that will shoot up in value) and sometimes

the cultural artefacts and stolen art or poached animal skins and horns that are sold to tourists in return for universally acceptable hard cash they can divert to their offshore tax havens or the on-shore properties registered under the names of maids and cats. (Crasta 2019, p. 127)

The EU Tran Committee research "Overtourism: impact and possible policy responses" defines that: "overtourism describes the situation in which the impact of tourism, at certain times and in certain locations, exceeds the physical, ecological, social, economic, psychological, and/or political capacity thresholds." (Peeters, et al. 2018, p. 15) The report goes on to describe how the travel trade considers overcrowding to be an issue that potentially constrains future growth, when in reality overtourism can pose an existential risk in more fragile cultural and natural heritage destinations. This can cause a decline in the quality of life of local residents due to increased costs of living and inflated real estate costs. Furthermore, overtourism can diminish a destination's authenticity and result in a deterioration of its attractiveness, eventually leading to a decline in its tourism appeal. Although overtourism is most often associated with cities, smaller islands, coastal and rural destinations are often more vulnerable to the impacts of overtourism owing to their limited infrastructure. This can result in a limited capacity to cope with a large influx of visitors within a short space of time. Furthermore, destinations in peripheral areas with a small population are likely to fall victim to overtourism more quickly owing to their limited ability to service and accommodate tourists and other visitors.

## Overtourism is Not a New Phenomenon

The reality is that, although, the term *overtourism* may be relatively recent, the phenomenon itself was recognized, at least in academic circles, as early as the mid-1980s when Jost Krippendorf's *The Holiday Makers* was first published. He commented as follows:

While the mid 1970s saw a growing interest in the impact of tourism on the environment, today (1984), when travel has become a mass phenomenon unequalled in history, people are beginning to discover the human dimension and the socio-cultural problems linked with increasing leisure time and mobility. This interest should have started much earlier. Indeed, this is where it should have all begun (Krippendorf 1984, preface).

He went on to describe how:

sensitivity to the negative effects of tourist mass migration is also beginning to develop in the local population in tourist areas. There is a growing feeling of literally being overrun and squeezed out by tourists. Don't we occasionally get the impression that local people are fed up with tourists.... (Krippendorf 1984, preface).

At the time, Krippendorf strongly encouraged destinations and policymakers to assess whether the current model and approach to tourism development and management had failed. To put *The Holiday Makers* into context it should be noted that there were only 318 million international tourist arrivals in 1985, which equates to around a fifth of the number recorded in 2019 by the UNWTO (UNWTO Tourism Dashboard | UNWTO 2020).

## Solutions to Overtourism Key to Long-Term Sustainability

It is clearly evident that the need to take action is no longer just urgent, but crucial if the travel and tourism industry is to become sustainable and deliver long-term tangible benefits to local people at the destination level as well as a positive experience for those visiting. It is encouraging to note that overtourism and sustainable tourism have finally reached the policy–agenda stage with governments and multilateral agencies recognizing the scale of the issue. For example, the EU Tran Committee research study suggests that the most relevant indicators of overtourism are as follows (Peeters, et al. 2018):

- Tourism density (bednights per km²) and intensity (bednights per resident);

- The share of Airbnb capacity of the combined Airbnb and booking.com bed capacity;
- The share of tourism in regional GVA; and
- Proximity to airports, cruise ports, and UNESCO World Heritage Sites.

According to the EU Tran Committee research study, these are considered preliminary indicators that destinations can use as a guide to establish whether they are at risk of overtourism (Peeters, et al. 2018, p. 16). However, this approach falls somewhat short as it does not take into account the impact of daytrippers, which are often considered to be a major cause of overtourism.

Dodds and Butler argue that the key to solving overtourism is to reduce tourist numbers and introduce mitigating policies such as un-promotion or de-promotion (Dodds and Butler 2019). Although this is perhaps feasible for individual destinations, it does not appear to be a realistic approach in the long term. Even in the current coronavirus pandemic environment, it seems highly likely that tourism will continue to grow long term as people will continue to view travel as an opportunity to enrich their lives, to escape, and to pursue happiness. Indeed, the travel bans and quarantines imposed in order to control the coronavirus pandemic led to significant pent-up demand as evidenced by post lockdown travel booking patterns in Europe. One of the biggest changes compared with the 1980s is that the media and a growing number of tourists are increasingly concerned about overtourism and overtraveling. Hopefully, this will result in more considerate tourist behavior in the future, especially in view of the coronavirus pandemic and the associated social distancing measures that have been introduced.

The Organization for Economic Co-operation and Development (OECD) considers that:

rethinking tourism success for sustainable growth requires a number of steps to be taken in order to understand more fully the impacts that tourism has on destinations, how to better manage increased visitor numbers as well as promote more sustainable and inclusive tourism development. Addressing these and other challenges faced by the tourism industry requires an integrated, forward-looking approach to policy formulation and implementation. Governments need new analysis, data and approaches that are calibrated to the fast-changing tourism sector. Tourism policy frameworks will need to be adapted to take account of and respond to these developments (OECD Tourism Trends and Policies 2020 | en | OECD 2020, p. 26).

At the national level, coordination measures are well-developed and long-term strategies are in place in many countries to optimize tourism's economic and social benefits, while minimizing the negative environmental impacts. The future challenge for many governments will be to ensure that any policy measures agreed upon at the national level can be consistently delivered at the regional and local levels. This will ensure that the local host communities in the regions where they are located can fully share the benefits of well-planned and managed tourism in the longer term. Tourism is of vital economic, social, and cultural importance to many countries and regions. As such governments have a key role to play in shaping tourism development in close collaboration with the local host communities and other key stakeholders.

It is important to recognize that overtourism is a complex phenomenon that can affect different types of destinations in a multitude of ways, which requires a bespoke approach in order to overcome the root causes and negative impacts. Root causes of overtourism may be due to fast expansion of the tourism sector combined with insufficient investment in tourism-related infrastructure. A rapid increase in air passenger arrivals or cruise ship calls can have significant impact on visitor flows at certain peak times in key public spaces. This may be exacerbated by technological advances such as social media coverage creating bucket list sites owing to their popularity on platforms such as Instagram, Facebook, Pinterest, YouTube, and TikTok. Research by the World Travel & Tourism Council (WTTC) showed that online reviews tend to concentrate on the most famous attractions with the top five attractions in Stockholm responsible for 42 percent of Tripadvisor reviews (McKinsey & Company 2017). Furthermore, peer-to-peer platforms such as Airbnb and Tripadvisor mean that tourists are increasingly visiting predominantly residential areas in order to get an authentic "live like a local" experience. This may create a more authentic experience for the visitors, but sometimes at the cost of local residents' privacy and in turn quality of life thereby having a negative social impact. Local residents feel intruded upon by tourists spending more time in "their" residential area.

The negative aspects of overtourism can manifest themselves in a number of different ways including environmental, economic, and sociocultural impacts. It is mainly the environmental and sociocultural impacts that have led to the increasing attention being paid to overtourism by the media, governments, local residents, and even tourists themselves in the recent past. However, the coronavirus pandemic and the absence of tourists have exposed the economic fragility of many destinations suffering from overtourism due to their overreliance on the tourism industry.

## Key Takeaways

- Overtourism can affect any type of destination: urban or rural, emerging or developed, but most frequently occurs in mature urban destinations.
- Overtourism occurs when the ratio between visitors and locals reaches a saturation point also known as the destination's carrying capacity.
- Overtourism is a complex phenomenon leading to negative sociocultural and environmental impacts.
- Overtourism is not necessarily about too many visitors overall, but rather in a specific location at a certain time.

# CHAPTER 2

# Overtourism in the Time of the Coronavirus Pandemic

## Introduction

This chapter discusses how the coronavirus pandemic became an opportunity for the tourism industry to reset at the destination level and in turn prevent overtourism from reoccurring or occurring in the first place. When the coronavirus began sweeping across the world in early 2020 no one was prepared for the profound impact it would have on the world economy and in particular on the travel and tourism industry.

## Overtourism and the Coronavirus Pandemic

On 24 March 2020, the World Travel and Tourism Council (WTTC) sent an open letter to the world's governments, revealing that more than one million tourism jobs globally were being lost every day as a result of the coronavirus pandemic. In November 2020, the total number of jobs estimated to have been lost was 142.6 million out of an estimated total of 330 million jobs in 2019 (Recovery Scenarios & Economic Impact from COVID-19 | World Travel & Tourism Council (WTTC) 2020). This demonstrates that the travel and tourism sector has faced an economic meltdown on an unprecedented scale. It will be a long struggle for the sector to recover and millions of people dependent upon it for their livelihoods have been plunged into debt and poverty.

According to the WTTC, growing job losses has affected the industry at every level with numbers increasing as more countries went in and out of lockdowns—with a "domino effect" as a consequence of temporary hotel closures, suspension of airlines, and a growing number of travel bans impacting the wider supply chain. In March 2020, Gloria Guevara, the president and CEO of WTTC stated: "No one can doubt that we are in unchartered territory—the coronavirus pandemic means the world is facing a threat on multiple fronts not seen previously in peacetime." The WTTC called upon governments of all countries to take immediate action to help ensure the survival of the job-creating sector that tourism is. Without prompt action it was clear that tourism-dependent economies around the world would face an existential threat. As of the beginning of 2021, it was thought that the most likely route to recovery, following the coronavirus pandemic, would involve people getting vaccinated combined with pretravel testing.

## Most Popular Tourist Destinations and COVID-19

It is interesting to note that a number of those destinations worst affected by the coronavirus pandemic in terms of deaths coincide with some of the most popular tourist destinations in the world. Some countries including the United Kingdom were slow to close their international borders and this may well have accelerated the spread of the virus in the early stages.

Table 2.1 illustrates that there is a strong correlation between the world's most visited countries and coronavirus-related deaths. This may be explained by the rapid growth in tourism and global mass mobility, particularly in urban areas, leading to the initial rapid spread of COVID-19. In this context, China and Thailand currently stand out as the countries that have been most capable of containing the spread of COVID-19.

Former UK cabinet minister and family doctor Dr. Liam Fox MP wrote in the *Sunday Times Magazine* on 22 March 2020 that "the struggle of the Chinese authorities to isolate and quarantine individuals in the current outbreak of coronavirus and its spread around the globe have shown the difficulties in trying to control infection when there are up to one million of us estimated to be travelling by plane at any given time" (Fox 2020). There were also concerns for a proportion of the projected 32 million passengers at sea worldwide that would be taking cruises in 2020, many of them elderly and therefore especially vulnerable to the virus. These estimates, of course, were rapidly downgraded by the travel industry amid the COVID-19 outbreak. Nevertheless, widespread and swift travel brought new problems in the handling of a pandemic crisis to which answers were needed.

*Table 2.1  Top ten international tourist arrivals and COVID-19 deaths*

| Country tourism ranking | Number of international tourist arrivals 2018 (millions) | COVID-19 deaths as of 31 December 2020 |
|---|---|---|
| 1. France | 89.4 | 65,037 |
| 2. Spain | 82.8 | 51,078 |
| 3. USA | 79.7 | 351,590 |
| 4. China | 62.9 | 4,785 |
| 5. Italy | 61.6 | 75,332 |
| 6. Turkey | 45.8 | 20,881 |
| 7. Mexico | 41.3 | 122,840 |
| 8. Germany | 38.9 | 35,574 |
| 9. Thailand | 38.2 | 3,532 |
| 10. United Kingdom | 36.3 | 75,024 |
| Total Top 10 Most Visited Countries | 576.9 | 805,673 |
| World Total | 1,409 | 1,826,852 |
| Share of World Total | 40.9% | 44.1% |

*Source*: UNWTO World Tourism Barometer, European Centre for Disease Control 2021

In March 2020, the coronavirus brought virtually all travel and tourism to a dramatic standstill. This put destinations previously facing overtourism in the unusual position of facing a major socioeconomic crisis. At the same time, the total absence of visitors, which previously were alienating local residents, provided destinations with a much-needed respite. Ironically, the tourism sector is uniquely placed to lead the recovery as it has the ability to provide the jobs required for the economy to bounce back and drive the growth needed for communities and countries to recover.

However, the coronavirus crisis created an opportunity for lessons to be learnt and to adapt new approaches to destination management. These include managing tourism in a more responsible manner in order to avoid overtourism and placing people at unnecessary economic, social, and environmental risk in the future. It is clear from the range of destinations that exists, that to avoid overtourism in future, requires a bespoke approach taking into account the unique characteristics of each individual destination. It will be easier to prevent the reoccurrence of overtourism than it will be to recover from it. Destinations across the globe have had an opportunity to reflect and reassess how a more effective destination management model can be put in place in order to ensure that overtourism does not reoccur. This will involve building destinations that are resilient in times of crisis and moving away from the traditional business model based on continuous global growth in international tourist arrivals.

## Coronavirus Pandemic an Opportunity to Pause and Reflect

The coronavirus pandemic highlighted that it is more important than ever to establish a set of baseline indicators for tourism at the local destination level. The coronavirus global crisis has provided an opportunity for destinations to pause and take stock of their tourism sector: which types of market segments, now absent, were the worst offenders with regard to overtourism? Which were the least and which actually helped and contributed in a positive manner? Destinations that were struggling to cope due to overtourism must now deal with the total absence of tourists and the economic repercussions resulting from this. Thus, now is the time for destination leaders, DMOs, key stakeholders, and local residents to plan for just how they wish their tourism sector to recover from the global health emergency caused by COVID-19. Destinations need to consider how tourism success should be measured in the future and they must move away from purely equating increasing tourist arrivals with success. Thus, destinations would benefit from referring to the Global Sustainable Tourism Council's (GSTC) minimum criterion:

> The destination should have an effective organisation, department, group, or committee responsible for the coordinated approach to sustainable tourism, with involvement by the private sector, public sector and civil society. This group should have defined responsibilities, oversight, and implementation capability for the management of socio-economic, cultural and environmental issues (GSTC Criteria | Global Sustainable Tourism Council (GSTC) 2020).

What will be the key lessons learnt from the coronavirus pandemic? Many destinations have already learnt that loss of overnight tourists hurt their economies several times more than the loss of cruise passengers or coach trippers on a day excursion. What businesses and types of tourism are destinations going to miss and what types of tourist should not be encouraged to come back? These are the sort of critical questions that need to be asked at the destination level. According to the UNWTO, many countries are highly dependent on tourism. In the Maldives around a third of GDP is derived from tourism, whereas in countries such as Spain and Italy tourism accounts for 15 and 13 percent of GDP respectively (UNWTO Webinar "Agenda 2030 and SDGs in times of COVID-19: the chance to true recovery"—Tourism for SDGs 2020). Being heavily reliant on the tourism sector can result in economic fragility. Thus, destinations should carefully consider how to develop a balanced economy, which probably means the tourism sector accounting for less than 10 percent of GDP.

The coronavirus pandemic should act as a reminder for destinations that it is more important than ever to manage the natural and cultural heritage resources that define a destination in a sustainable manner in order be resilient and future proofed. One of the positive outcomes from the coronavirus pandemic was that the public and private sectors had to collaborate more closely in order to best prepare themselves for the recovery phase. This was an opportune time for destinations to reflect and take action in order to be well placed for the long and challenging road to recovery. Destination communities around the world had experienced their places void of tourist crowds but at the same time faced growing economic hardship. What type of tourism would they choose in the future and how should it be managed? Consumer research indicated that in the initial stages of recovery tourists would seek to visit places that are uncrowded—this could either be close to home domestic destinations or further away remote international destinations. It also seems that people are likely to travel less often but for a longer period of time based on the principle of making trips that matter as well as financial considerations for some.

In August 2020, the WTTC recognized the need for concerted international leadership to combat COVID-19 and to ensure that the road to recovery is as short as possible and to minimize the devastation caused by the pandemic. It has identified four key measures to help the travel and tourism industry to recover (ICC and World Travel & Tourism Council issue COVID-19 restart guide for the Travel & Tourism Sector 2020):

1. Wearing a mask
2. Testing and contact tracing
3. Quarantine for positive tests only
4. Reinforcing global protocols and standardized measures

WTTC research indicated that even a modest resumption in domestic and international travel and tourism can bring significant economic benefits and safeguard jobs. However, the current lack of consistency and stop–start approach in terms of protocols, quarantine measures, announcements, and measures introduced by different countries is not helping restore people's confidence in traveling again and adapting to the new reality (ICC and World Travel & Tourism Council issue COVID-19 restart guide for the Travel & Tourism Sector 2020).

## Overtourism Challenges

The previous information was, of course, a completely different rhetoric to the messaging in WTTC's publication: *Coping with Success Managing Overcrowding in Tourism Destinations* (McKinsey & Company 2017) stating that:

> The Travel and Tourism sector is a cornerstone of our global economy—and thanks to a growing middle class, improved digital and physical connectivity, and generations of people with an insatiable appetite to explore the word, it is expanding rapidly. Such growth is accompanied by a number of challenges, many of which can be summed up with the term overcrowding which is by no means new, but which has been coming to a head in popular destinations across the globe in recent years.

According to the WTTC, the challenges facing the tourism industry include (McKinsey & Company 2017):

**Overcrowding is a complex issue:** The problems associated with overcrowding can vary, from alienated local residents to overloaded infrastructure. The issues can affect both established and emerging destinations of all kinds. Countries, regions, cities, and individual sites, such as parks, beaches, and museums, may all be affected.

**Diverse interests are involved:** Stakeholders including governments, comprised of elected officials and national, regional, and local agencies; tourism management and promotion agencies; commercial organisations, ranging from multinational corporations to locally-owned small businesses; those employed in the sector; local residents; non-profit and social sector organisations; and finally; tourists themselves. Given the diversity of these stakeholders' objectives and interests, not all solutions work for everyone.

**Thorny questions of ethics and values are embedded**: 'Value over volume' is a focus for many destinations. But is it reasonable to reduce visitor numbers to a more sustainable level if that action also makes the destination accessible only to the wealthy? What of the view, espoused by some, that travel is a basic right? These are difficult questions, and we cannot presume to answer them on anyone's behalf. But neither can we ignore them.

The previously mentioned issues will need to be addressed by destinations as part of their recovery response to the coronavirus pandemic. Especially, if destinations wish to emerge stronger, more resilient and sustainable.

## Key Takeaways

- Global travel and tourism sector came to complete stand-still between March and May 2020 due to travel restrictions implemented during the coronavirus pandemic that has had devasting impact.
- The pause in international tourism has exposed the economic fragility of destinations previously suffering from overtourism being over reliant on the travel and tourism industry.
- Destinations now have the opportunity to decide how they wish to recover and regenerate post the coronavirus pandemic and which visitors to focus on in the future.

# CHAPTER 3

# The Exponential Rise in Global Tourism Leading to Overtourism

## Introduction

This chapter highlights how the exponential rise in global tourism is considered one of the main causes of overtourism. The unprecedented growth in international tourist arrivals over the last five decades combined with rapid growth in domestic tourism means that more people than ever before are traveling across the globe. The almost continuous growth in international tourism has led to demand challenges resulting in overtourism in an increasing number of destinations. Tourism went through an almost total global shutdown due to the coronavirus pandemic, something which would have been unimaginable at the beginning of 2020. However, as a number of vaccines became available in early 2021, travel is expected to gradually resume to previous levels with recovery anticipated to take around five years.

## Fifty Years of Growth in International Tourism

After 50 years of more or less continuous growth tourism came to a sudden halt in March 2020 due to the coronavirus pandemic. International tourism started again slowly in July 2020, with the European Union (EU) keen to restart travel owing to its economic importance and to avoid a total collapse of the sector. However, this was on a phased basis with the European Commission highlighting the need for the sector to re-emerge as safer from a health perspective and more sustainable from an environmental perspective. Social distancing measures will inevitably require better destination management in locations prone to overtourism. As of

December 2020, the majority of travel was either domestic or short-haul intraregional trips. However, newly identified COVID-19 strains resulted in more travel restrictions being introduced, with global mass vaccination leading to herd immunity considered the only realistic road to recovery for the travel and tourism sector.

The exponential growth in international tourist arrivals from around 25 million in 1950 to almost 1.5 billion in 2019 and forecast to increase to 1.8 billion by 2030, pales in comparison to the sheer size of domestic tourism, which is expected to reach 19 billion by the same year. While the overtourism debate tends to focus on international tourism, it is important to recognize that the scale of domestic tourism means that it remains the leading form of tourism and has the potential to play a fundamental role in regional and local economic growth and development.

Until recently, tourism was considered a luxury reserved for the select few who could afford both the time and money to travel. Increased leisure time, higher incomes, and global mass mobility have led to more people than ever being able to travel. Enhanced air connectivity, the expansion of accommodation, the growth in all-inclusive packages, and other forms of relatively affordable leisure travel have exponentially increased the opportunity to travel for leisure purposes. Today, tourism is no longer reserved for the few, but is considered a right for an ever-increasing number of people. Furthermore, people are taking more frequent and shorter breaks including city breaks and weekend breaks often due to the availability of cheap flights and affordable accommodation. The shorter length of stay means that people tend to pack it all in, in order to see all the key attractions in the shortest possible time leading to a concentration of tourist flows both in terms of time and space. The availability of digital maps, social media, and peer-to-peer review sites makes it easy to navigate and decide which "must see" attractions to visit.

This phenomenal story of growth has resulted in tourism being recognized as one of the fastest growing and most important economic sectors in the world. In 2019, the WTTC estimated that the sector contributed nearly USD8.9 trillion to the global economy equating to 10.3 percent of global GDP. In the same year, the travel and tourism sector was responsible for circa 330 million jobs or one in ten jobs around the world. Furthermore, WTTC statistics show that the travel and tourism sector

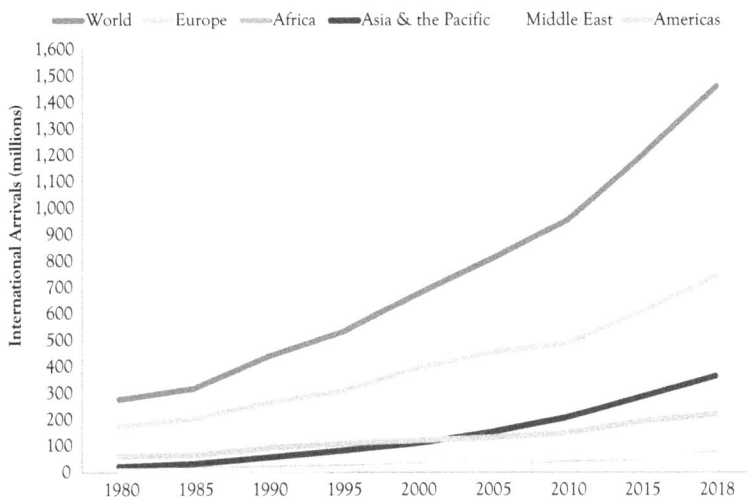

*Figure 3.1 World tourism arrivals (1980 to 2018))*

*Source:* UNWTO 2020

outpaced global growth for the years 2009 to 2019 (Travel & Tourism Economic Impact | World Travel & Tourism Council (WTTC) 2021).

The above chart shows the evolution in international tourist arrivals from 1980 to 2018 by region (see Figure 3.1).

It is evident from Figure 3.1, that Asia and the Pacific and Europe have seen the largest increases in absolute international tourist arrivals since 1980. This led to the occurrence of overtourism in an increasing number of places around the world, especially in some of the world's honeypot sites ranging from Venice in Italy to Angkor Wat in Cambodia.

Typically, overtourism occurs when the ratio between tourists and locals reaches a pinch point and the destination becomes saturated. In essence, a destination becomes too popular which in turn leads to its decline. The level at which a destination becomes saturated and the local host population starts to feel that the quality of life is impacted negatively is largely based on social perception and will vary from destination to destination, but it is currently the most prevalent in mature European destinations.

## Current Trends in International Tourism

Destinations worldwide received almost 1.5 billion international tourist arrivals in 2019, up 3.6 percent on the previous year according to the UNWTO. 2019 was another year of strong growth, although, slower compared to the exceptional rates of 2017 (+6 percent) and 2018 (+6 percent). In 2019, demand was slower mainly in advanced economies and particularly in Europe. All regions enjoyed an increase in arrivals. The Middle East (+8 percent) led growth, followed by Asia and the Pacific (+5 percent). International arrivals in Europe and Africa (both +4 percent) increased in line with the world average, while the Americas saw growth of 2 percent. As per the main source markets, France reported the strongest increase in international tourism expenditure among the top ten markets, while the United States led in absolute terms (UNWTO Tourism Dashboard | UNWTO 2020).

Based on recent trends (i.e., prior to the coronavirus pandemic), economic prospects and the UNWTO Confidence Index, the UNWTO was forecasting growth of 3 to 4 percent in international tourist arrivals worldwide in 2020. This has since been adjusted downward in the wake of the coronavirus pandemic. According the UNWTO international arrivals fell by more than 70 percent during the first ten months of 2020, which translated into a loss of USD935 billion in export revenues, which was ten times the loss resulting from the 2009 global financial crisis (Tourism Back to 1990 Levels as Arrivals Fall by More than 70 percent, 2021). Putting this into context, the UNWTO noted that in 2009, on the back of the global economic crisis, international tourist arrivals declined by 4 percent, while the SARS outbreak led to a decline of just 0.4 percent in 2003. These numbers are based on the latest developments as the global community faces up to an unprecedented social and economic challenge and thus should be interpreted with caution in view of the extreme uncertain nature of the coronavirus crisis.

## Rapid Growth in Tourism Exposing Inadequate Destination Management

According to the OECD, continued growth in international tourist arrivals has raised important questions as to how best to manage growth to benefit people, places, and businesses. The over-riding issue for governments, and increasingly society, is to better look after the assets on which tourism depends. This is relevant to all destinations, but is a particularly pressing issue in those experiencing overtourism where significant invest-ment may be required to preserve and protect the natural and cultural heritage assets as well as to develop visitor-related infrastructure (OECD Tourism Trends and Policies 2020 | en | OECD 2020).

Pavia Rosati, who founded the travel site Fathom, stated that (Froelich 2020):

> the Italian government needs to start restricting the number of visitors allowed into Venice on a daily basis…and probably do a better job of restricting—or even banning—the floating mall-sized cruise ships that disgorge tens of thousands of people into the city, making its narrow streets un-passable for Venetians who are just trying to get home from work. If this unwanted forced reset helps us get smarter about our limited resources and be a little selfish about how we behave when we go out into the world, we will come out of this crisis in a better place.

During the height of travel restrictions and lockdowns associated with the coronavirus pandemic, the canals of Venice became clear for the first time in centuries with dolphins and swans returning, due to the absence of the steady stream of cruise ships. But the local people working in tour-ism, who were already suffering from the *acqua alta* flooding in Novem-ber 2019, suffered the financial repercussions of COVID-19, which have reminded many how vital tourism is to the economy. On one hand, local residents had a much-needed break from overtourism and from the reality of being a living museum. On the other hand, the *Sunday Times* reported that as of mid-August 2020 the continuing lack of cruise ships had a detrimental impact on the livelihoods of those whose jobs depend on the 30 cruise operators usually based at the city's maritime terminal. This highlights the contradiction between local residents with no vested inter-est in tourism and those whose livelihoods depends on it (Conradi 2020).

Prior to the coronavirus pandemic overtourism together with the cli-mate emergency had become major challenges facing the tourism industry, albeit these are topics that the industry had been aware of for at least a few decades. The concept of a destination's carrying capacity was first raised in the 1980s and later defined by the UNTWO as "the maximum number of people that may visit a tourist destination at the same time, without causing destruction of the physical, economic, socio-cultural environment and an unacceptable decrease in the quality of visitors' satisfaction" (Risks of Saturation of Tourist Carrying Capacity Overload in Holiday Destinations (English version | World Tourism Organization 1983). However, this definition is not as comprehensive as the following: "the level of human activity an area can accommodate without the area deteriorating, the resident community being adversely affected or the quality of visitors' experience declining" (Hawkins and Middleton 1998). Each destination will have an individual carrying capacity in terms of how many visitors it can handle in order to avoid overtourism. This will depend on its characteristics, be it an urban or rural location as well as the size of the local host population for example. In the context of overtourism, the social and psychological carrying capacity is most relevant as this is a good indicator of the local host population and community's perception of overcrowding and congestion caused by tourism. Key to understanding the social and psychological carrying capacity of any destination is engaging with the local host population and community on a regular basis so that measures can be taken to avoid overtourism from occurring. It is also important to bear in mind that overtourism often occurs in densely populated and heavily congested urban spaces with growing populations and housing shortages, which may be exacerbated by the growth in tourism. It is clear that understanding a destination's carrying capacity is a complex issue, especially in urban areas, based on the social, psychological, environmental, and economic factors that require regular monitoring.

While the short-term outlook for tourism is extremely uncertain, the industry is likely to continue growing in the long term. At present, the international tourism landscape is facing an unforeseen existential challenge and this together with the prevalent political, environmental, and digital trends will require destinations to consider the implications in order to inform future tourism policy. Early indications suggested that one of the likely short-term outcomes of the coronavirus pandemic was growth in domestic tourism as local lockdowns were lifted gradually. People visited destinations closer to home that were considered to be safe, hygienic, and clean without facing the risk of having to quarantine upon their return from abroad.

## Key Takeaways

- Tourism has experienced unprecedented growth for the past five decades becoming a key economic driver across the world.
- Long-term growth is expected to reach 1.8 billion international trips and 19 billion domestic trips by 2030.
- The travel and tourism industry is expected to recover from the devastating impact of the coronavirus pandemic within five years.
- Travel is an aspirational activity and people will travel as and when they can.
- DMOs should anticipate such growth and plan accordingly.

# CHAPTER 4

# Key Factors and Trends Affecting Tourism Growth Leading to Overtourism

## Introduction

This chapter highlights some of the key factors and trends that have affected tourism growth. Global mass mobility, digitalization, new technology, the 2008 global economic crisis, terrorist attacks, changing behavior, and preferences among travelers have had a profound effect on the global tourism industry over the last two decades. The coronavirus pandemic accelerated technological changes and digitalization as the world adapted to the "new normal."

## Affluence and Aspirational Travel—the Key International Source Markets

Tourism remains an aspirational activity and people will continue to travel as and when they can. The world's population has also expanded rapidly leading to increased urbanization and population density. Thus, in many ways, the evolution of tourism has just begun. Global mass mobility is here to stay and, although, the way people travel may change due to the effects of the coronavirus pandemic it is unlikely to dampen growth in the longer term.

As of the end of August 2020, Euromonitor International estimated that the travel and tourism industry will experience a long-lasting negative economic impact across the entire tourism value chain and that recovery will take between five and ten years depending on the sector (Travel 2040: Sustainability and Digital Transformation as Recovery Drivers 2020). Therefore, destinations should use this time to plan for recovery and regeneration toward a more sustainable tourism model.

Table 4.1 shows that the top ten international source markets were responsible for 46.2 percent of total international tourism expenditure in 2018. It should be noted that with regard to China only a relatively small proportion (around 150 million) of the total population traveled internationally in 2018, which explains why the expenditure per capita is so low. Prior to the onset of the coronavirus pandemic, Chinese travelers were forecast to take 160 million trips abroad in 2020, making them the fastest-growing international source market in the world. In contrast Germans took 109 million outbound trips in 2018 indicating that most of the population travels abroad at least once a year. Global tourism receipts have more than tripled since 2000 and currently account for around 7 percent of global exports and services making tourism the fifth largest traded services sector (UNWTO Tourism Dashboard | UNWTO 2020).

Prior to the onset of the coronavirus pandemic, Euromonitor International anticipated that the global travel and tourism industry would continue to power on and expected the sector to grow by 3.3 percent year

*Table 4.1 Top ten international tourism spenders 2018*

| Top ten international tourism spenders 2018 | Expenditure USD (billion) | Population 2020 (million) | Expenditure per Capita USD | Market Share % |
|---|---|---|---|---|
| China | 277 | 1,438 | 193 | 8.2 |
| United States | 144 | 331 | 436 | 7.7 |
| Germany | 96 | 84 | 1,142 | 7.0 |
| UK | 69 | 68 | 1,016 | 4.9 |
| France | 48 | 65 | 734 | 4.0 |
| Australia | 37 | 26 | 1,451 | 3.2 |
| Korea | 35 | 51 | 684 | 3.2 |
| Russia | 34 | 146 | 235 | 2.8 |
| Italy | 30 | 61 | 498 | 2.6 |
| Spain | 27 | 47 | 573 | 2.6 |
| World | 1,398 | 7,775 | 180 | 100 |

*Source:* UNWTO 2020

on year in constant terms, forecasting it to top more than £2.3 trillion by 2024. It is estimated that online sales currently account for just over half of all sales (52 percent) with mobile sales representing a quarter of all travel bookings in value terms as the travel industry continues its digital transformation (The Impact of the Coronavirus on the Global Economy | Market Research Report | Euromonitor 2020).

The world's population is becoming increasingly affluent. It is estimated that a billion more people will be in the global middle class by 2030 (Bremner 2019). With travel becoming ever more accessible, the sector is likely to continue to grow at unsustainable levels in the longer term once the global economy recovers from the coronavirus pandemic. The anticipated growth in tourism demand will be driven by rising incomes in emerging markets making travel more accessible to a wider range of audiences, causing an 8 percent annual growth compared to the 4.3 percent growth of international arrivals. The average spend per arrival is expected to hold up to price pressures and will marginally increase to £854 by 2024, up from £844 in 2019, which points to a shift toward higher spending per trip as destinations transition toward a more sustainable tourism model (Bremner 2019).

The coronavirus pandemic forced governments and destinations to take stock and re-evaluate the economic benefits and in many places the necessity of the tourism sector, while at the same time considering the potential of the tourism sector to enhance the quality of life and wellbeing of the local community. Questions have been raised as to whether destinations really wish to go back to business as usual including rapid growth and high volumes of low-value visitors, lack of investment in infrastructure, and little consideration for the local host community and natural environment. According to the Travel Foundation:

> this seems unlikely given the risks of future pandemics, geo-political uncertainty, dwindling resources and climate change. While issues of overtourism and unchecked growth may now seem a distant memory, the "weight" of tourism will return, and with it, renewed pressure on destinations struggling to cope or trying to figure out what their own growth trajectory may look like (Sampson 2020).

The task of rebuilding tourism presents a once-in-a-lifetime opportunity to move away from the previous paradigm of a focus on ever-increasing visitor numbers and tourism receipts, while the needs of local communities and the natural environment were poorly served. According to the Travel Foundation, now is an opportune time to reverse this pattern and place local communities and the resources they depend at the heart of the recovery planning (Sampson, 2020). To achieve this will require strong destination management, which focuses on collaboration between the local community, residents, and key stakeholders in order to maximize the positive benefits of a thriving tourism sector.

It is important to remember that the travel and tourism industry also has many positive impacts that are less frequently mentioned in the media. These include, an often significant, contribution to local employment, investment in public infrastructure, wildlife conservation as well as protection of natural and cultural heritage assets. The negative social and environmental impacts caused by overtourism tend to arise when destinations become over reliant on the travel and tourism sector and are not well managed. Effective destination management is critical to ensure that the tourism industry achieves a sensitive balance that delivers economic prosperity at local level, but at the same time is also socially and environmentally sustainable.

## Rapid Growth in Air Travel

The world has become more accessible through more frequent and cheaper air transport, which has led to global mass mobility. According to the International Air Transport Association (IATA), international air transport grew at double-digit rates from its earliest post World War II days until the first oil crisis in 1973 (IATA, History—Growth and Development 2021). Much of the growth impetus came from technical innovations such as the introduction of turbo-propeller aircraft in the early 1950s, transatlantic jets in 1958, wide-bodied aircraft and high by-pass engines in 1970, and later advanced avionics. These advances brought higher speeds, greater size, better unit cost control and as a result, lower real fares and rates. This combined with an increase in real incomes and more available leisure time led to an explosion in the demand for air travel as illustrated in Figure 4.1.

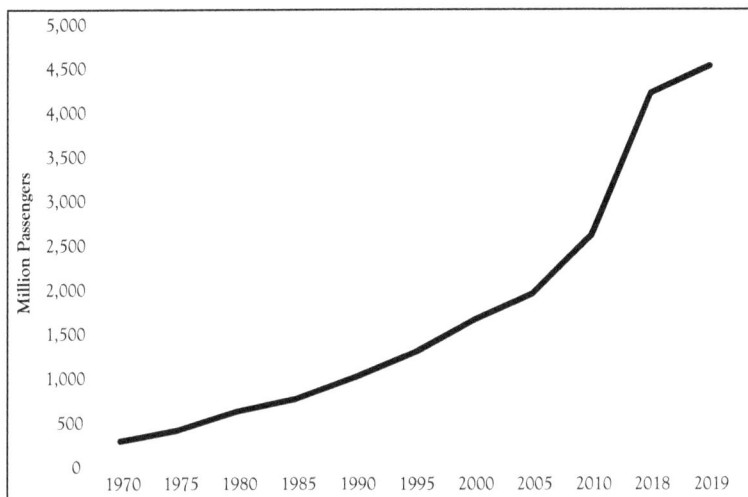

*Figure 4.1  Global air passengers (1970 to 2019)*

Source: Worldbank 2020

At any given moment in 2018, an estimated 1.4 million people were airborne on a commercial flight somewhere in the world (Fox 2020). Most were on a short-haul flight linked to a nearby city within the same country as evidenced by the most densely trafficked sector: the 454-km hop from Seoul to the resort island of Jeju, off South Korea's southern coast. Another major factor influencing the growth in air travel, especially short haul, has been the advent of low-cost airlines such as Southwest Airlines and easyJet. In Europe, the phrase "easyJet Generation" refers to young people who have grown up in a region where cheap aviation and open borders have permitted unprecedented mobility. Since the 1990s the world has seen more people flying than ever before and the act of flying has become a core lifestyle practice leading to global mass mobility. Global mass mobility, due to access to frequent and cheap flights, is considered one of the major causes of overtourism.

While the 20th century saw the creation and rapid growth of the international air transport industry, the beginning of the 21st century was marked by great challenges met with major transformations. Over the last two decades, the aviation industry has been challenged by a number of crises and shocks including terrorism, volcanic eruptions, global economic crisis, and pandemic threats. In spite of setbacks the growth in air travel continued at an exponential rate fueled by developing economies, such as Brazil, Russia, India, and China (BRIC countries) with improved access and an ever-increasing middle class. Growth is unlikely to level off until these become mature markets. Of course, growth in air travel will continue to be affected by unanticipated shocks such as the coronavirus pandemic, which will have a major short-term impact. However, looking at how the industry has recovered and continued to grow following previous crises events, air travel is likely to bounce back strongly following the current upheaval. For example, the relative drops in passenger traffic were deepest following the combined 2000 to 2001 shock of the dotcom bust and the terrorist attacks of 9/11, and the 2008 shock of the global financial crisis. According to the World Economic Forum, traffic had returned to its trend level within four years continuing to grow in line with the long-term trend. Indeed, after the 2008 financial crisis, tourism was seen as a key driver of economic growth and in turn wealth creation (Calderwood and Soshkin 2019). It is clear that the coronavirus pandemic had a very severe impact on international travel as countries introduced international travel restrictions and bans in order to contain and minimize the spread of the virus.

Historically, the airline industry has been able to adapt its operations and business models in response to crises and external shocks. It cannot be taken for granted that resilience will be automatic. There is a counter argument that air travel will take longer to recover from the coronavirus pandemic and that the quantity and range of flights will shrink considerably especially to smaller regional destinations. It is unlikely that airlift will be restored to the level of 2019 for a number of years. The majority of airlines have been devastated and as a consequence will become smaller. They have had to cut routes which in turn will impact hotels and other tourism-related businesses. Many faced bankruptcy and ceased trading due to lack of cashflow resulting from reduced demand as the pandemic continued to bite. At the end of 2020, the International Civil Aviation Organization (ICAO) estimated that the coronavirus pandemic had resulted in air travel demand dropping by 2.89 billion travelers and that gross passenger operating airline revenues fell by as much as USD181 billion during 2020 (ICAO 2021). The limitations resulting from less air capacity are likely to protect destinations against overtourism in the short to medium term with overtraveling reduced due to higher airfares and less airlift capacity.

## Growth in Cruise Travel

Similar to the growth in air travel, the rapid evolution of the cruise industry has had a major impact on destinations and has increasingly caused congestion in the most popular destinations ranging from Venice to Santorini and from Dubrovnik to Reykjavík.

As early as in the 1850s, ships catering purely for passengers were firmly established but it was not until the 1880s that the concept of cruising took off when ships such as the Mauritania, Lusitania, Olympic, and the ill-fated Titanic were introduced (Smith 2021). These large ships were purpose-built and offered a wealth of luxuries similar to those found in a five-star hotel. In keeping with the time, a class system was established onboard for passengers who mainly traveled for business or immigration purposes. Despite the Titanic's fate and World War I, cruising began to rise in popularity during the 1920s and 1930s. However, the introduction of air travel by jet after World War II meant that traveling by ship was no longer popular. It was not until 1974 when Cunard revolutionized cruising with the introduction of large-scale entertainment including cabaret acts, international celebrities, high-end production shows, and extensive dining options for leisure purposes that cruising really took off. At the same time, shore excursions were introduced meaning that cruising became a holiday rather than a way of getting from A to B. Unlike other modes of transport, the cruise ship itself became the core element of the holiday experience (Smith 2021).

Since the late 1960s the growth in the number of cruise passengers has been uninterrupted even during the global financial crisis in 2008 to 2009 and the Costa Concordia loss in 2012 off the coast of Isola de Giglio in Tuscany Italy. This incident led to a period of negative PR for the industry (Neate and Bowers 2012). As the fastest growing segment of the travel industry, cruising has come a long way since the 63 passengers that sailed on the Britannia in 1840. In 2010, Royal Caribbean launched the biggest cruise ship in the world the "Allure of the Seas," which has a 6,000-passenger capacity with facilities more akin to a floating city (Allure of the

Seas 2021). Ships are becoming ever larger and more innovative in terms of the facilities and services offered with an average capacity of over 3,000 passengers. The enormous size and capacity of modern cruise ships has a major impact on the destinations visited such as small islands, which can become overwhelmed quickly when thousands of daytrippers descend on a destination within a short space of time.

As may be seen from Figure 4.2, the global cruise industry has expanded rapidly over the past three decades. The number of cruise passengers increased by a compound annual growth rate of 6.6 percent between 1990 and 2018 from 3.8 million to 28.2 million (CLIA 2020).

Some of the most popular cruise regions around the world are North America, the Caribbean, and Europe. The Mediterranean and its adjoining seas have been a major driver of cruise passenger growth over the past two decades (Pallis 2015). As a consequence, cruise ports and destinations face a number of challenges due to the increasing number of passengers arriving, particularly in Europe. While the economic benefits, in terms of spending in destinations can be significant, especially in turnaround ports where cruise passengers join or depart the cruise and therefore tend to stay overnight. However, the sheer volume of cruise passengers descending on

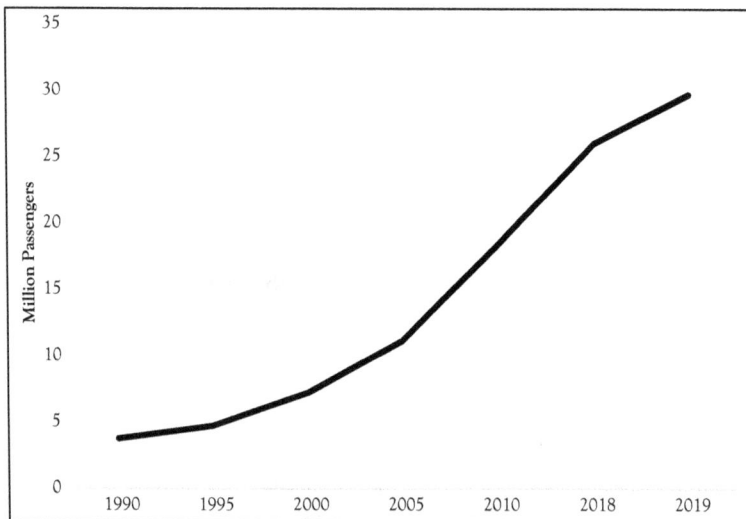

*Figure 4.2 Cruise passenger evolution (1990 to 2019)*

*Source:* OECD and Cruise Lines International Association (CLIA), 2020

destinations in large groups during the day throughout the main summer season (from May to October in Europe) is increasingly causing friction with local residents due to congestion and overcrowding.

There are different views as to how the cruise industry will emerge post the coronavirus pandemic with some suggesting that people will be extremely reluctant to go on a cruise, especially as the main demographic for cruises tends to coincide with those most vulnerable to succumb to COVID-19. On the other hand, some cruise operators have reported a major increase in forward bookings in 2020 compared with the previous year. This would suggest that avid cruisers are not too concerned about taking a cruise in the future. Undoubtedly, cruise operators will innovate quickly to improve safety and hygiene standards for passengers, and this may indeed happen more rapidly than at the destination level. Thus, passengers may feel more secure staying on a ship than in a local unbranded accommodation establishment that may not meet the same safety and hygiene standards.

## Tackling Overtourism Caused by Cruise Passengers

Venice is one of the most popular home ports (Conradi 2020) in the Mediterranean and is well-known for the negative effects caused by overtourism. In 2014 a ban was imposed on large cruise ships passing through the center of Venice, preventing all ships over 96,000 gross tons from sailing the city's main cruise terminal as well as limiting the number of bigger ships to five a day. Local residents had protested that the presence of the larger ships was increasing pollution and speeding up the erosion of the UNESCO World Heritage city's medieval buildings that are sinking into the lagoon surrounding Venice. In August 2019, the Italian minister for transport went further and announced that cruise ships would be routed away from the center of Venice to the outlying terminals of Fusina and Lombardia. The decision followed an incident in June 2019 where a cruise ship hit a dock in the city (Roberts 2019). Four people were injured when the ship crashed into a dock and a tourist river boat on the Giudecca Canal, one of the busiest canals leading to St. Mark's Square.

An access fee of up to €8 for day-trippers was due to be introduced in July 2020 in Venice as the city struggled to manage a tourism industry that sees around 26 million visitors per annum, many arriving by cruise ship. The revenue generated by the fee will be earmarked for public services impacted by tourism such as rubbish collections and street maintenance while locals will see their taxes reduced at the same time. The fee will be collected at the main entry points to the city, which in turn will provide important footfall and tourist flow data for future reference. The entry fee for daytrippers has been temporarily scrapped until July 2021 due to the coronavirus pandemic as the city of Venice is now suffering serious financial problems due to the lack of tourism, the main source of income for the city. This demonstrates the economic fragility of a destination that is overly dependent on tourism. Some had been arguing that the introduction of an entry fee for daytrippers was too little too late and that the city needed a more proactive approach to sustainable tourism in order to ensure that locals benefit from the industry. The coronavirus pandemic provided an opportune time for Venice to consider the best way forward while tourism was temporarily on hold.

In an attempt to tackle overtourism, Dubrovnik in Croatia is due to introduce a maximum limit of 4,000 cruise passengers to be allowed ashore daily and from 2022 each will face a charge of €2. The UNESCO World Heritage site known as the "Pearl of the Adriatic" has been struggling with an increasing number of cruise visitors, partly due to the success of Game of Thrones, which was filmed in the city and most of the locations can be visited in a day making it an ideal shore excursion (Connolly 2019). In 2018, Dubrovnik received around three million visitors mainly from about 400 cruise ships that docked at the harbor. It is evident that such a large influx of daytrippers is causing long-term damage to the city's historical sites while the cruise ships create water, air, and noise pollution affecting the marine ecosystem adversely (Connolly 2019). In addition to the daily charge to be imposed on cruise passengers, Croatia has established a Tourism Development Fund to facilitate the development of public infrastructure in support of visitor attractions in less developed areas and is taking steps to encourage new segments seeking different types of experiences (OECD Tourism Trends and Policies 2020 | en | OECD 2020). However, there is evidence to suggest that once one destination introduces measures to reduce overtourism then tourists move on to the next destination. In the case of Dubrovnik that may mean Kotor in nearby Montenegro.

On a more positive note, smaller, often more exclusive, expedition cruises tend to be more considerate of local culture and the environment. The Association of Arctic Expedition Cruise Operators (AECO) was founded in 2003 and is an international organization for expedition operators who are dedicated to managing responsible, environmentally friendly, and safe tourism in the Arctic—the core areas being Svalbard, Jan Mayen, Greenland, Arctic Canada, the Russian Arctic National Park, and Iceland (AECO 2020). The members agree that expedition cruises and tourism in the Arctic must be carried out with the utmost consideration for the vulnerable natural environment, local cultures, and cultural remains, as well as challenging safety hazards on sea and on land. Members encourage incorporating specific standards and guidelines for operating expedition cruises in the Arctic. Furthermore, it recommends the use of highly qualified guides and staff knowledgeable and experienced in the Arctic environment, its natural and human history and contemporary culture. The AECO network currently includes 76 members, 40 passenger vessels, and 10 yachts, which handled over 25,000 expedition cruise passengers in the Arctic in 2018 (AECO 2020). The polar expedition cruise industry is expanding with 30 new vessels anticipated within the next five years with advanced vessel structure and technology, new operators, and new itineraries. Among Arctic expedition cruise destinations, the most visited is Svalbard while Alaska and Iceland are already seeing a large number of expedition and conventional cruise passengers. Clearly future growth will represent challenges in the Arctic which AECO's members are anticipating and seeking to mitigate through better research to inform knowledge-based tourism management.

Cruises are seen by many as being worse than "all-inclusive" holidays as they encourage mass tourism due to the sheer number of passengers on each ship, which in turn can lead to overtourism. Passengers typically spend little money in the destinations they visit as excursions are paid for as part of the cruise package and not at the destination level. Destinations need to proactively manage and segment cruise ships in order for the sector to work optimally in terms of maximizing socioeconomic benefits. Environmentally fragile niche destinations such as Svalbard, Greenland, and the Faroe Islands need to carefully consider what types of cruises they want, when, and how many in order to maximize the economic impact and minimize any negative impacts such as environmental degradation caused by large volumes of cruise passengers all arriving during a short period of time. This can be particularly overwhelming in sparsely populated remote locations. The work of AECO demonstrates that a carefully managed cruise industry can be positive as long as the scale and size of ships are appropriate to avoid congestion and pinch points arising. Small expedition-style cruises a la Compagnie du Ponant can accommodate visitors to more remote areas such as Svalbard and Greenland, which are difficult to access and offer limited tourist accommodation on land. Such remote and inaccessible places have difficulty in sustaining visitor numbers year-round, which means that investment in onshore tourist accommodation is often not viable. The main value is in offering imaginative and innovative excursions that involve and benefit the local community.

The Svalbard Environmental Protection Fund was established in 2007. The fund's primary source of income is an environmental tax of NOK150 levied on everyone visiting Svalbard. The fee is automatically added to the ticket price, so the majority of tourists are unaware of it (AECO 2020). This seems a missed opportunity to communicate and promote the important role and work of the fund. Today, the fund supports projects and interventions to conserve and protect the natural and cultural environment of Svalbard of around NOK 20 million per annum (AECO 2020). The purpose of the fund is not to facilitate the growth of tourism, but rather to help mitigate any negative environmental impacts caused by tourism and other traffic. Grants are also provided to support research and studies to identify and monitor the environment and causes of environmental impacts as well as to inform, educate, and facilitate environmental protection in the broadest sense.

## Major Drivers of Overtourism

As described in the previous sections, the exponential growth in international air and cruise passengers is a major contributory factor to the rise in overtourism. Responsible Travel considers the real cause of overtourism to be the collusion between airlines, cruise ships, and governments to create artificially cheap flights and cruises at the expense of taxpayers and the environment. For example, it is not uncommon today to be able to purchase a short-haul European flight to Barcelona for less than the cost of a meal out. It is worth noting that in 1944 the aviation industry sealed a deal known as the Chicago Convention that made aviation fuel exempt from tax (Frances 2020). Similarly, the cruise industry uses one of the cheapest types of diesel known as "bunker" fuel. This type of fuel is highly polluting and causes public health risks and thus would not be allowed on land. It enables cruise lines to keep costs low and invest in ever larger new ships. However, destinations such as Copenhagen who are proactively looking to tackle climate change are seeking to make it mandatory for cruise liners to use sustainable sources of power while docking at Copenhagen Malmø Port (Wonderful Copenhagen 2020).

Iceland is a prime example of how the combination of growth in visitors arriving by air and cruise have been a major contributory factor to overtourism, particularly in Reykjavík during the peak summer season. Iceland has a small population of just over 364,000 of which the majority 233,000 live in the Reykjavík capital region (Statistics Iceland 2021). Iceland was at the center of the global financial crisis in 2008 when its banks failed leading to a collapse of the housing market and a tripling in unemployment resulting in a bailout by the International Monetary Fund (IMF) (Sheivachman 2019). A weakening of the Icelandic Krona made Iceland more affordable to travelers and this combined with the eruption of Eyjafjallajökull in 2010 made Iceland a global tourism hotspot in large part due to excellent airlift via the national carrier Icelandair. In 2019, Iceland received just under two million international visitors arriving by air through its main hub Keflavík Airport—this was decrease of 14.2 percent on the previous year—but still almost a quadrupling from just over half a million in 2001. The decrease in international tourists in 2019 was due to the strong Krona making Iceland more expensive and the collapse of budget carrier WOW. In addition, cruise passenger arrivals at Reykjavík have increased at an even faster rate from around 28,000 in 2001 to 144,000 in 2018 (Statistics Iceland/Visit Iceland 2020). This combined with the coronavirus pandemic meant it was a good time for Iceland to pause and take stock on the future shape of its tourism industry.

Warnings about overcrowding were voiced as early as 2011 and as tourism continued to grow rapidly overtourism became a reality in Iceland. Its relatively small host population has been struggling to cope with an ever-increasing influx of visitors despite the economic boost the tourism industry provided. Icelanders were rightly concerned about this and there was a growing feeling that as the industry matured, it was time to decide how tourism could become more sustainable in the long term. In 2018 to 2019, destination management plans were published for the seven regions in Iceland with a view to establish a DMO in each with a view to improving the coordination of tourism priorities and regional development as well as act as a support unit for data collection, innovation, product development, skills, digitalization, and marketing (OECD Tourism Trends and Policies 2020 | en | OECD 2020).

## Consequences of Growth in International Travel

The continued growth in international travel has raised questions around how travel and tourism can best be managed to the benefit of all people, places, and businesses. While at the same time mitigating any adverse impacts on the cultural fabric, natural, and built environment in destinations across the world. The OECD advocates that:

> there is a need to rethink tourism success for sustainable growth. In particular, it encourages policy makers to take steps to help destinations avoid pitfalls, as they strive to strike a balance between the benefits and costs associated with tourism development and implementing a sustainable vision for the future (OECD Tourism Trends and Policies 2020 | en | OECD 2020, p. 11).

So, while overall growth in tourism is considered positive by the OECD, it also recognizes that governments increasingly need to develop urgent policies that seek to maximize the economic, environmental, and social benefits while at the same time seeking to reduce the negative impacts and pressures that can arise when growth is unplanned and unmanaged.

## Social Media and Technological Advances

The digital revolution has been a significant contributor to the growth in tourism in terms of changing the way people travel and purchase services as well as how products are promoted and advertised. Trends include an increased use of online resources and mobile platforms to source information when planning a trip, be it websites or social media, combined with a decreasing use of offline sources such as brochures and travel guides. Advances in online booking platforms, peer-to-peer review sites, and online guides and mapping tools have made traveling much easier and faster as these allow tourists to pick up information quickly about top local attractions and current activities, which in turn may stimulate hot spots and overcrowding. The EU Tran Committee research study on overtourism identified such technologies as having the potential to accelerate growth in volumes and tourist flows in some locations leading to overcrowding and in turn overtourism (Peeters, et al. 2018, p. 24).

Furthermore, social media and other technological advances such as artificial intelligence and machine learning are driving travel and tourism behaviors of the millennial generation. In particular, the "bucket list" is a major trend focusing on visiting the most accessible and renowned sites, which can lead to overtourism if visitor flows are not managed effectively. It is crucial for destinations to be aware of as well as value and protect their "bucket list sites," which tend to be the most appealing attractions that can quickly become congested and fall victim to overtourism. Social distancing measures introduced during the coronavirus pandemic will likely mean that destinations will be quicker to introduce technological monitoring to ensure that key locations do not become overcrowded. For example, destinations can learn from museums and visitor attractions, which track visitor numbers and sell timed tickets to avoid overcrowding at peak times. Equally, such an operating system can be applied to public spaces and cultural events.

## Sharing Economy

The "sharing economy" is perhaps the most significant trend to emerge over the past decade with the emergence of new online digital platforms for short-term rentals such as Airbnb and HomeAway as well as the more recent inclusion of short-term rentals on platforms such as Booking.com. This has resulted in the market growing at an unprecedented rate and outpacing the growth of traditional modes of tourist accommodation including hotels and guest houses. With the help of new technologies, the traditional cost of doing business has decreased significantly enabling both private individuals and smaller commercial enterprises to partake.

Consumers increasingly value experiences such as travel. Apart from value for money, consumers seek authentic, local, and unique experiences. These trends have led to the phenomenal success stories of sharing economy brands like Airbnb in addition to a growing interest in activity-based travel according to Euromonitor International (Geerts 2020). Tourists are increasingly in search of authenticity and unique experiences, which sometimes mean "discovering" lesser-known neighborhoods and destinations in order to live like a local. According to the EU Tran Committee research study evidence, there is a correlation between a high number of Airbnbs in residential areas and increasing negative social impacts associated with overtourism such as noise (Peeters, et al. 2018). The arrival of Airbnb has exposed poor regulations and control of the local housing market in a number of destinations. This in turn has exacerbated the issue of too many tourists in local residential areas. However, Airbnb has recently stated its commitment to collaborate with DMOs and local authorities to ensure that local housing markets are not distorted by short-term holiday lets.

In the case of Copenhagen, it is thought that the DMO Wonderful Copenhagen's desire to deliver local authentic experiences could be at the expense of locals. This was highlighted by Lonely Planet suggesting that the city had fallen victim to overtourism with local residents increasingly concerned about the growing number of visitors and increasing noise levels (Brady 2019). Like many other popular European cities, Copenhagen has experienced a meteoric rise in overnight tourist arrivals increasing by 74 percent over the past decade and reaching 8.8 million overnight stays in registered accommodation in 2018, excluding an estimated 1.9 million Airbnb stays. On top of this comes cruise passengers of which there were 868,000 in the same year as well as other daytrippers (Brady 2019). Wonderful Copenhagen is forecasting that the number of tourist arrivals will double by 2030 to reach an estimated 16 million overnight stays. However, part of the future strategy "10xCopenhagen" is based on a two-pronged approach to disperse visitors better throughout Copenhagen and the northern part of Zealand as well as by season. Geographically,

**VESTERBRO**

Not long ago, Vesterbro's primary claim to fame was its status as the red-light district of the city. Today, the area is packed to the brim with top-drawer restaurants, cafés and hip bars – especially in the now so famous Meatpacking District. By day, the old butcher halls are filled with CrossFit buffs sweating along, start-ups disrupting, world-class coffee brewing and restaurants serving the packed sidewalks. By night, the neon lights turn on, and the area becomes the beating heart of Copenhagen's nightlife scene. Vesterbro is undeniably cool and mixes its colourful history and gritty vibes with modern metropolitan life as lived by local families and light-hearted partygoers.

*Figure 4.3  Billboard promoting the Vesterbro area of Copenhagen*

Source: Helene Møgelhøj, Copenhagen Airport August 2020

Copenhagen is divided into a relatively compact central city area as well as five adjacent outer areas where the majority of the local population live, all offering a distinct neighborhood feel. Vesterbro home to the red-light district and the former meatpacking area is a case in point as may be seen from Figure 4.3.

For many years the majority of tourists visiting Copenhagen would only have visited the city center, but this is starting to change due to the DMO's successful efforts to get people to visit other parts of the city in order to enjoy a local and authentic experience as well as a rise in the number of Airbnb properties available. These are typically situated in the outer areas as this is where the biggest concentration of local housing is found as shown in Figure 4.4.

However, Wonderful Copenhagen and the City Council are well aware of the issues and frequently engage with the local community and other stakeholders so that issues are addressed on an ongoing basis to ensure that any negative impact on the residents' quality of life is minimized. This is backed up by research, which suggests that 67 percent of local residents in Copenhagen experience no problems with the city's

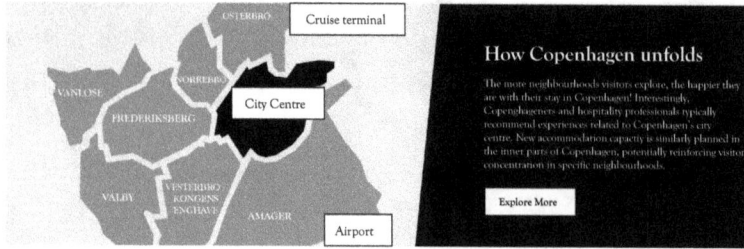

*Figure 4.4 Map of key areas and locations in Copenhagen*

Source: 10xcopenhagen.com 2020

tourism and overall remain positive about welcoming even more visitors to Copenhagen in the future. Only 6 percent of those surveyed cited that there were often problems due to tourism in the city including noise, traffic congestion, and litter/waste (10xCopenhagen 2020). Indeed, Wonderful Copenhagen, has a dedicated project manager tasked with sustainable tourism development in the city.

Unusually, for a DMO, Wonderful Copenhagen's 10xCopenhagen strategy includes a substantial focus on Copenhageners' perception and experience of tourism in their daily lives, in addition to research on the competitive position of Copenhagen's tourism product as well as the future drivers of tourism growth (10xCopenhagen 2020). The strategy makes the following recommendations in order to make the city even better:

- Create a program to develop decentralized tourism strategies and measures of success, cocreated between the local community, local industry, city and tourism developers. Address more aspects of the value creation of tourism—with relevance and direct impact on local lives.
- Make channels available for Copenhageners to identify and voice tourism-related issues and opportunities on an ongoing basis.
- Establish a task force to address top locations or aspects of the locals' experience of tourism-related traffic issues (10xCopenhagen 2020).

The strategy goes on to suggest ways to make Copenhagen expand to accommodate the anticipated increase in the number of tourist arrivals.

- Include sustainable tourism growth as a relevant element in urban planning, as well as a positive tool to strengthen the appeal of more city areas and neighborhoods to locals and visitors alike.
- Consider new ways to incentivize investment and initiatives that spotlight Copenhagen as an attractive destination beyond the center of the city.
- Develop visibility and visitability of attractions outside the inner-city area, using a lighthouse strategy to make experiences around attractions more accessible to visitors.
- Enable better, broader, and more personal recommendations where credibility and opportunity exist (within hospitality, events, transportation, etc.) (10xCopenhagen 2020).

## Airbnb

At the end of 2020, Airbnb was represented in more than 100,000 destinations and over 220 countries with total worldwide listings in excess of 7 million facilitated by around 4 million hosts (Airbnb 2020). Airbnb has been the subject of much discussion in relation to overtourism over the last couple of years as well as accused of causing rising rents and housing shortages for local residents as professional landlords chose short-term Airbnb rentals over long-term local tenants. Furthermore, most hoteliers tend to view Airbnb as an unregulated operator selling tourist accommodation at a low price, thus distorting the traditional visitor accommodation environment in any given location. Tourist boards and traditional hoteliers warn that there is no safety, quality control, or brand reassurance and the owners may not be paying sufficient tax. Of course, the arrival of Airbnb has exposed the inherent weaknesses of poorly regulated and controlled housing markets in destinations around the world leading to rents and real estate prices being inflated driven by professional landlords letting multiple properties and in turn contributing toward overtourism.

Mainly, Airbnb has been treated a bit like an OTA (online travel agent), that is, a very successful and disruptive booking engine undermining the traditional accommodation sector distribution channels. In reality Airbnb is so much more than that. Yes, for some it may be about finding a bed or a room at the lowest price in the right location, but it can be argued that for many consumers it is about much more. This is frequently illustrated by the no end of fashionable social media influencers and bloggers staying in a diverse range of unique and photogenic Airbnbs across the globe confirming the often not insignificant visual appeal of the properties on offer. In fact, Airbnb is not particularly fast and efficient when it comes to making a booking, as this often requires a fairly extensive dialogue with the owner before any confirmation is made. Both parties can ask questions and look at each other's profiles and reviews prior to making a commitment. Like Uber, Airbnb is rooted in the sharing economy, which is driven by technological platforms that have enabled worldwide sharing of services between people who do not know each other at a relatively low cost. Thus, at its core Airbnb is about sharing travel experiences and spaces for mutual economic benefit. It is not about a cookie cutter quality-controlled and brand-reassured homogenous experience, but rather about engaging with local people in their environment, because usually the host is more than happy to introduce guests to their favorite places within their local community. In essence local people become the destination's ambassadors. Obviously, this also has a downside as this means more tourists end up staying in what are predominantly residential neighborhoods such as in the Copenhagen case described earlier.

Despite all the warnings millions of hosts and consumers have bought into the Airbnb concept, so it is clearly working regardless of the criticisms. If nothing else, it has certainly acted as an innovation stimulant in the more traditional accommodation sector. Indeed, boutique and luxury hotel brands have started using guided selling tactics that blend content and personalization to foster a deeper engagement with the destination and encourage direct bookings.

However, the coronavirus pandemic means that many of the "so-called" professional landlords have switched to other platforms aimed at longer rentals, which are likely to be more beneficial to local residents. According to *Wired*, the city of Prague used the coronavirus pandemic as an opportunity to take back control of its short-term rental market in order to increase the supply of housing available to local residents (Temperton 2020). No doubt other major cities will follow suit in order to try and redress the balance between short-term visitor accommodation and housing for local residents. It is likely that the coronavirus crisis will result in a much leaner Airbnb, which will hopefully be more aligned with the original vision and getting back to its roots of providing short-term accommodation with an opportunity to live like a local and engage with the local community. Indeed, in an interview with the *Sunday Times Magazine*, one of Airbnb's founders Brian Chesky recognized some of the mistakes made by Airbnb and apologized with a promise to reset and go back to the "roots, back to basics, back to what is truly special: everyday people who host in their homes" (Arlidge 2020).

According to the Dutch Review, Amsterdam banned Airbnb from 1 July 2020 in certain central parts of the city in order to avoid returning to the overtourism experienced prior to the coronavirus pandemic. In other parts of the city Airbnb will continue to be allowed subject to a special permit and for a maximum of 30 days per annum for groups of no more than four people (Lalor 2020). These measures are widely supported by the stakeholders and the local community with 75 percent of the 780 inhabitants and organizations surveyed in favor. The coronavirus pandemic has provided local people with an opportunity to get to know their city and its neighborhoods without tourists and with a lot less noise, something the authorities are keen to preserve going forward.

Lisbon has taken a different approach to ensure that local housing stock is no longer primarily used as Airbnb rentals. Up to a third of the housing in Lisbon's historic core was used by Airbnb prior to the coronavirus pandemic. Fernando Medina, the city's mayor, has utilized the coronavirus crisis to ensure a proportion of Airbnb-style properties are turned into affordable "safe rentals" for local people including key workers and the elderly who are often threatened with eviction and faced with having to move out of the city center (Medina 2020). In 2020, the city offered to pay landlords, many of whom had mortgages to pay but few visitors, to turn Airbnb-style rentals into safe rentals thereby prioritizing affordable housing and protecting local communities as well as the city's unique character. This is not intended to turn future tourists away, but rather to improve local people's quality of life in Lisbon with a view to creating a more vibrant, healthier, equitable, and in turn greener city by reducing local residents' need to commute. Landlords will be required to sign two- to five-year leases and are unlikely to be able to return to letting their property to tourists even in the long term.

It seems that Airbnb is not the root cause of overtourism and displacement of local residents although it may have been a contributory factor. In fact, this has more to do with regulation and control of local housing markets where weaknesses with regard to subletting have been exposed and taken advantage of by landlords and tenants. This is something Airbnb is fully aware of and has vowed to tackle in collaboration with city councils and DMOs.

## Authenticity and Experiential Travel in a Digital World

In recent years, there has been a growing demand for adventure and experiential travel with tourists seeking out unusual and unique experiences. On the whole consumers, especially millennials, are looking for more authentic experiences that connect with the local community in terms of arts, culture, and gastronomy thus providing a more memorable personalized experience. In general, the goal of experiential travel is to have an immersive experience and gain a fuller understanding of the destination. Experiential travel is closely linked to the search for authenticity and localism. Technology and sharing economy platforms have provided people with the tools to plan and design their own trips and experiences. It is not surprising that destinations such as Iceland have seen growth in visitor numbers due to this trend, as it offers a plethora of outdoor activities from heli-skiing to glacier and volcano hiking and from whale watching to horse trekking, providing a wide variety of experiences in a short space of time to some of today's cash-rich time-poor travelers. Furthermore, many experiential experiences are provided by passionate innovative entrepreneurial micro and small businesses making them a great way to engage with the local host population.

Recent research by the European Travel Commission emphasized the importance of pursuing hobbies and interests as a driver of tourism, with gastronomy, adventure, urban experiences and "living like a local" resonating with most visitors (European Travel Commission 2019). In terms of gastronomy, travelers are keen to seek out hidden gems such as places that have long been favorites among locals and offer sought-after home-grown flavors. Advances in digital technologies and social media have made it much easier to discover and share such experiences.

The digitalization of travel and tourism was initially thought to encourage wider dispersal of visitor flows. In reality, it has turned out differently due to the powerful influence of social media, which has had a homogenizing effect stimulating the desire to visit bucket list destinations from Italy's Venice to the Lima's Machu Picchu and from the Great Wall of China to Nepal's Mount Everest, resulting in overtourism in an increasing number of destinations. According to the WTTC 2018 report on overtourism this trend is particularly pronounced among first-time international millennial travelers who use social media to show off (McKinsey & Company 2017).

In the case of Nepal, the effects of overcrowding have been deadly as reported by the Guardian newspaper on May 11, 2019, 11 climbers died attempting to reach the Mount Everest Summit owing to more than 100 climbers queuing up to ascend the crest (Gentleman 2020). According to experienced mountaineer Nirmal Purja:

> such bottlenecks have been troubling the mountain with increasing frequency. The deaths were not caused by the queue itself, but a different problem: the rising numbers of inexperienced climbers who view Everest as the ultimate selfie destination, and the proliferation of companies willing to take their money and let them have a go, regardless of their ability.

This despite the USD11,000 permit required to climb the mountain, and package prices ranging from around USD30,000 to USD200,000. In 2019, 381 permits were issued, an increase of 35 over the previous year. The Nepalese Government is fully aware of the situation and are considering introducing more stringent measures to ensure that people issued with a permit are physically capable of reaching the summit as well as restricting the number of climbers that can attempt the summit on any given day (Gentleman 2020). However, the coronavirus pandemic has left Nepal's tourist industry devastated and may have reduced the Government's willingness to impose more robust regulations at least in the short term. Many of the cooks, porters, and guides whose livelihoods depend on the climbers were left with no income and have had to return to their villages due to the absence of tourists.

Until recently, the impressive chalk cliffs at Seven Sisters were mostly known for Beachy Head's unfortunate reputation as a suicide spot and being a popular site for local ramblers. The iconic Seven Sisters' wall of chalk is located within the South Downs National Park in East Sussex, England. Today, Seven Sisters is world famous due in no small part to the power of social media. According to an article in the *New York Times* the cliffs have become extremely popular with Chinese and South Korean visitors after being featured on an online travel site popular with younger Chinese travelers as well as in a video featuring a South Korean actress standing close to the cliff edge (Tsang 2018). Asian visitors primarily come to the UK to visit London and imagine that Seven Sisters is close by, when in reality it is at least a two-hour journey to reach them from the capital. They come to visit mainly because they have seen Seven Sisters appear on social media or in films, especially Harry Potter and Atonement, and by recommendations from celebrities. The rapid influx in visitor numbers from Asia is both an opportunity and a threat. On the one hand if they can be persuaded to stay longer and spend money locally that is a good thing, but on the other hand they are putting increasing pressure on the fragile cliffs, which often experience cliff fall due to erosion making it dangerous to go close to the edge. In 2017, a tourist sadly died after losing her footing too close to the cliff edge.

It is worth noting that during the first weekend in May 2020 after easing of the coronavirus lockdown in England, Seven Sisters was flooded with visitors, and local residents were quoted stating that they had never experienced so many visitors before (BBC news 2020). This illustrates that overtourism is not necessarily caused by foreign visitors, nor by overnight tourists, but can indeed also be caused by domestic daytrippers who may spend very little in the destination visited. In fact, most cases of overtourism are caused by a combination of international and domestic day and overnight visitors, which highlights the need for destinations to carry out regular visitor surveys and monitoring in order to segment their visitors and tailor destination management strategies and actions accordingly.

# Sustainability

The "Greta effect," named after the Nobel Peace Prize winning teenage Swedish activist Greta Thunberg who became the face of the Generation Z environmental movement, means that sustainability has risen toward the top of the travel and tourism agenda. Globally, the tourism sector accounts for up to 5 percent of carbon emissions according to the UNWTO (Euromonitor 2019). The "Greta effect" is stimulating positive changes in attitudes and behavior both at the destination and the consumer level with an increased desire to find solutions to mitigate the negative impacts of tourism on people and the environment.

The coronavirus pandemic has provided people with time to reflect on their travel behaviors and to experience an extended period without the opportunity to travel for nonessential purposes. This has not dampened the overall desire to travel and experience other places and cultures, but perhaps rather highlighted the need to make travel matter and to take fewer but more meaningful journeys involving flying. Having experienced less noise and air pollution for a period of time while facing higher prices and increased waiting times at airports due to stringent health checks and quarantine measures, people are thinking twice about embarking on, yet another short-haul city break to a potentially overcrowded urban destination.

The term *flygskam* (or flight shaming) as the Swedes call it seems even more relevant now. This is likely to result in more staycations involving travel by train or car. Carbon reductions and sustainability were becoming critical issues for the travel and tourism industry prior to the coronavirus pandemic with customers increasingly expecting measures to be in place without necessarily being willing to pay for these. Conde Nast Traveller is advocating that "it is time to make a practical and personal shift to travel better—better for communities in the places we visit, better for us to connect with destinations in positive and meaningful ways, and better for the natural world." Conde Nast Traveller's ten ways to be a better traveler post the initial coronavirus pandemic lockdown include (Mathieson 2020):

1. Take more staycations
2. Buy fewer toxic travel products

3. Rethink flying
4. Consider slow travel
5. Consider locals
6. Stay at hotels rooted in the community
7. No more animals
8. It's not just about the carbon footprint
9. Travel to the right destinations
10. Aim for low-volume tourism (Mathieson 2020)

A similar message is promoted by the WTTC who recommends that individuals consider the following points to become more responsible and sustainable travelers (WTTC 2017):

- **Educate:** Spread your knowledge and approach by making responsible tourism choices.
- **Talk:** Share with others and use their knowledge to increase your own.
- **Learn:** Develop curiosity about the ways you can be part of the solution.

Consumer research by Euromonitor International indicates that consumers are particularly conscious of social and environmental sustainability with an elevated focus on inclusivity and localism (Euromonitor 2019). Although, consumers are increasingly aware of sustainability and responsible travel it seems that there is a disconnect with the vast majority of travel and tourism operators who are not engaging to the same extent with the sustainability agenda. In general, the travel and tourism industry has been slow to respond to the changing consumer preferences.

From a destination management perspective tourism has a vital role to play in achieving the United Nation's (UN) 17 Sustainable Development Goals (SDGs) as highlighted by the UNWTO, the United Nations Development Programme (UNDP) and the UN. These organizations recommend that destinations and tourism stakeholders take action to accelerate the shift toward a more sustainable tourism sector by aligning policies, operations, and investment with the SDGs (UNWTO 2020).

The most significant SDGs in relation to tourism are SDG 8 (Decent Work and Economic Growth), SDG 12 (Responsible Consumption and

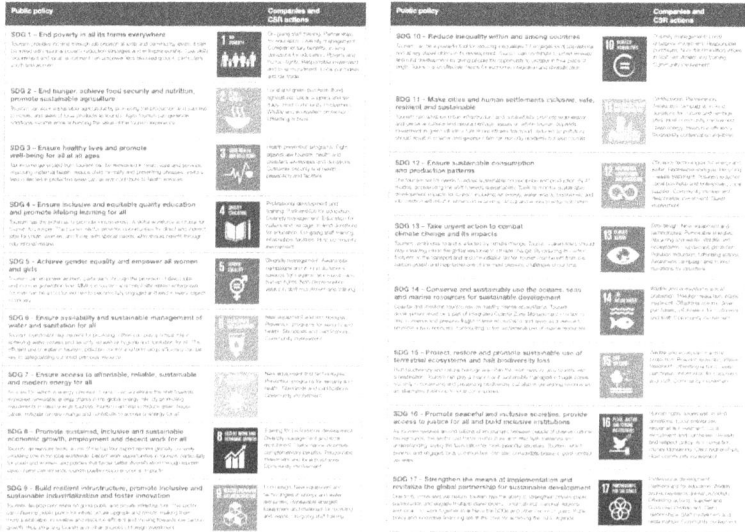

**Figure 4.5 Tourism links with the SDGs: public policy and business actions**

*Source:* UNWTO 2017

Production), and SDG14 (Life below Water). Although, owing to the travel and tourism sector's link with other sectors and industries it can accelerate progress toward all 17 SDGs. The SDGs and their relevance to tourism destination management and development are listed in the Figure 4.5 prepared by the UNTWO (UNWTO 2020).

The second version of the GSTC's Destination Criteria has been updated to reflect the 17 SDGs and how a destination can contribute toward the 2030 Agenda for Sustainable Development (GSTC 2020). Against each criterion, one or more of the 17 SDGs is identified, to which it most closely relates. According to the GSTC, the criteria relate to a place, not a body; however, many of the criteria may be taken up by a DMO to ensure a coordinated approach to sustainable destination development. Overall, the criteria are structured in the following four areas providing a range of indicators to be complied with for destinations to achieve the accreditation:

### 1. Sustainable management
- Management structure and framework
- Stakeholder engagement
- Managing pressure and change

## 2. Socioeconomic sustainability
- Delivering local economic benefits
- Social wellbeing and impacts

## 3. Cultural sustainability
- Protecting cultural heritage
- Visiting cultural sites

## 4. Environmental sustainability
- Conservation of natural heritage
- Resource management
- Management of waste and emissions (GSTC 2020)

It is clear that the coronavirus pandemic has provided destinations and DMOs with time to reflect on how best to recover and regenerate from the devastating coronavirus pandemic. This should help guarantee that the tourism industry emerges stronger, more sustainable, and resilient in order to ensure that the local host population derives maximum benefits without facing overtourism in future.

## Staycations and Localism

According to Wikipedia a staycation, or holistay, is a period in which an individual or family stays home and participates in leisure activities within driving distance of their home and does not require overnight accommodation. They tend to increase in popularity during periods of uncertainty and economic crisis. The term *staycation* is now used widely not only in the United States and UK, but also throughout mainland Europe.

In the UK, where the staycation phenomenon first emerged following the global financial crisis in 2008 to 2009, it is defined as a holiday taken in the UK by British residents and includes all holidays away from home whether that be a day trip, weekend break, a two-week holiday, or a shorter retreat with more than half of all adults in the UK staycationing in 2017. According to research by Visit England the latest available figures show that there were 59m staycations in the UK in 2017; an increase of 6 percent over 2016. Total spend reached £23.7 billion, up 3 percent in 2016 (Visit England 2017).

On the surface, it may appear that the staycation is a simple substitution, with people switching to a holiday at home rather than going abroad.

However, research by Visit England suggests that it was more complex than that. The growth in domestic holidays was not purely driven by necessity, but also by a group called "extras." Extras may be described as those who started taking more domestic holidays while cutting back on international travel, but at the same time driven by a growing interest in localism and authenticity.

Staycations typically include city breaks, cultural holidays, culinary and spa holidays, which are less seasonal and therefore more likely to be taken throughout the year. Destinations that are able to create itineraries around these themes are likely to be able to stimulate visitation outside the peak season. Clearly, staycations are set to become even more popular following the coronavirus pandemic as they do not tend to involve flying nor traveling abroad. Indeed, many prefer to stay hyper local in the short term, only traveling relatively short distances by car or train. Staycationers are also likely to seek out local food and drink as well as local art and cultural experiences.

Although, it was expected initially that many British residents would choose a staycation over traveling abroad during summer 2020, the early indications were not very clear. Early data analysis by Visit Britain (Visit Britain 2020) suggested that self-catering in rural and coastal areas performed very well. However, hotels and other serviced accommodation in city centers and urban areas continued to suffer and as of the end of 2020, it did not look like the recovery would be rapid due to the continued absence of international and business travelers. Ongoing changes to quarantine and self-isolation measures resulted in significant delays with regard to the resumption of international travel. However, the arrival of a number of COVID-19 vaccines toward the end of 2020 was a cause for optimism with regard to the return of international travel in 2021.

## Second City Traveler

Booking.com is predicting the rise of "the second city" traveler, meaning the exploration of lesser-known destinations in a bid to reduce overtourism and protect the environment, will take a leap forward in the coming years. Second city travelers are keen to swap destinations if they may lead to less of an impact on the environment or indeed would have a positive impact on the local community. The coronavirus pandemic also made consumers focus more on rural as well as sun and beach destinations where social distancing can be practiced with relative ease as opposed to more densely populated urban centers.

The coronavirus pandemic accelerated the pace of technological trends that were already happening with online and virtual becoming more important than before as well as the desire to explore destinations closer to home.

## Key Takeaways

- The rapid growth in international air travel and cruise over the past five decades are major contributory factors in overtourism.
- Increasing affluence and aspirations will continue to drive growth in international travel in the long term.
- The sharing economy, social media, and other technological advances are driving growth sometimes leading to the creation of bucket list hotspots.
- The demand for local, authentic, and experiential travel can sometimes result in tensions with the local host population.
- Increasing consumer awareness of sustainability, especially social and environmental, but so far businesses have been slow to respond.

# CHAPTER 5

# Tourism Destination Development Evolution and Lifecycle

## Introduction

This chapter focuses on how destinations evolve through various lifecycle stages as the tourism sector develops and grows before eventually entering a stage of stagnation or even decline if not managed effectively.

Destinations are at different stages of the lifecycle from emerging to high-growth destinations and from mature destinations to destinations in decline due to, for example, overtourism and lack of investment in tourism-related infrastructure. As described in previous chapters, overtourism can affect all types of destinations including cities, coastal, rural, countryside, and protected landscapes as well as in developed versus developing countries at different stages of the lifecycle. Although, overtourism most frequently affects mature urban destinations that are close to reaching a saturation point or their carrying capacity.

## Destination Evolution and Lifecycle

The idea of destinations entering decline due to overtourism is not new and was highlighted by Butler in his Tourism Area Life-cycle Model in 1980 (see Figure 5.1). Butler not only described how the authenticity and quality of the visitor experience declines in line with rapid growth in visitor numbers, but also how the local host population's attitude to tourists is likely to change over time. This is particularly true when a destination is close to reaching its carrying capacity or saturation point.

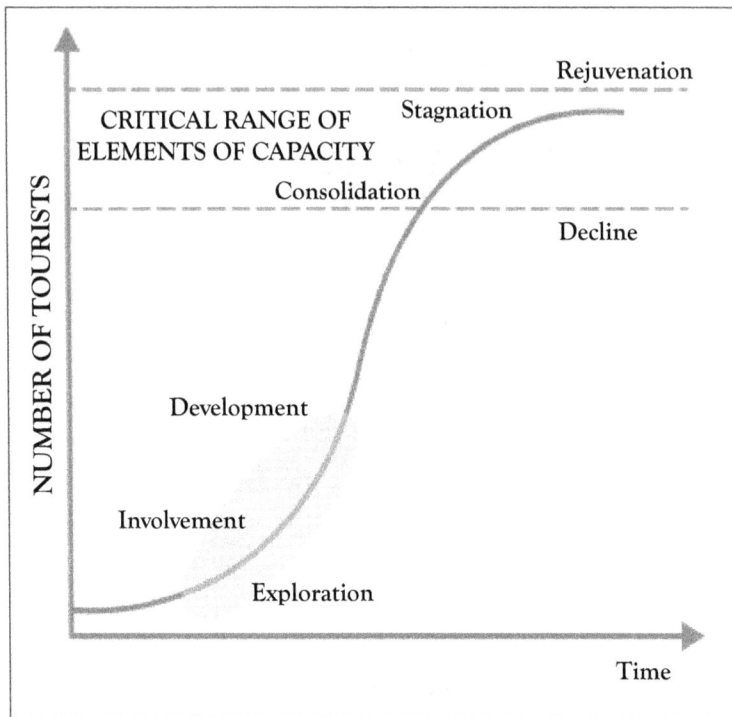

*Figure 5.1 Butler's tourism area lifecycle model*

Source: R W Butler, Canadian Geographer, 1980

As may be seen from Figure 5.1, Butler's model identifies five key destination lifecycle stages:

1. **The exploration stage**—an emerging destination with its tourism industry in a state of infancy with limited tourism-related infrastructure and most tourists may be described as "explorers" (Butler 1980). There are very few of these remaining today as tourism has grown exponentially since 1980, but perhaps the Pitcairn Islands may be considered to fit into this category.

2. **The involvement stage**—a destination with an increasing number of tourists that attracts local and public investment in infrastructure (Butler 1980). The small island of St. Helena in the South Atlantic has a population of just over 6,000 and may be described as being in the involvement stage, given the public sector investment of

circa GBP286 million in the airport (St. Helena Enterprise 2019). Until 2018, St. Helena could only be accessed by a monthly ship from Cape Town, which involved a trip lasting at least three weeks including the roundtrip journey to and from South Africa. The island now has an airport offering a couple of flights a week via Johannesburg or Cape Town. In 2018, St. Helena attracted around 3,000 overnight staying visitors with the number of future tourists currently capped at 30,000 per annum. The future of tourism in remote destinations such as St. Helena is inextricably linked to the capacity, frequency, reliability, and cost of flights to the island, so in theory the number of tourists can be controlled with relative ease. With no scheduled flights to St. Helena owing to the coronavirus pandemic, tourism is currently on hold as of January 2021.

3. **The development stage**—a period characterized by increased foreign direct investment and a range of visitors and market segments, driven by heavy marketing and promotion. The population in the destination accepts tourism (Butler 1980). Myanmar is an example of a destination in the development stage. Compared with its neighbours of Thailand, Vietnam, and Cambodia there are relatively few international visitors at just 4.5 million in 2019 (tourism.gov.mm 2021). This means there is significant untapped potential, which to date has attracted some foreign direct investment. However, unlike in Butler's description Myanmar has not been heavily promoted at this stage, but this is partly due to the changes in how emerging destinations are marketed in an increasingly digital world, which did not exist in 1980, as well as the increase in global mass mobility.

4. **The consolidation stage**—the main income of the local economy comes from tourism, and visitor levels continue to increase but at a decreasing rate. Extensive marketing and promotional efforts are made to overcome seasonality and to develop new markets. The local people fully appreciate the importance of tourism. The growth rate begins to slow (Butler 1980). Boracay in the Philippines is an example of a destination that had nearly reached saturation, but where the local authorities decided to take decisive action before it was too late and closed the island for six months to carry out a comprehensive environmental clean-up. Since reopening, the num-

ber of tourists has been restricted to a maximum of 6,400 people on island per day and they are obliged to stay in accredited accommodation only (Jennings 2019).

5. **Stagnation stage**—occurs when visitor numbers peak, carrying capacity is reached, and the area is no longer trendy. There are fewer first-time visitors, and the destination relies on repeat visits and conventions for business. At the stagnation stage a destination either enters a decline or is rejuvenated subject to appropriate intervention and effective destination management (Butler 1980). Barcelona is a good example of a destination having reached the stagnation stage or its carrying capacity with the city experiencing the effects of overtourism owing to a large influx in cruise passengers and MICE (Meetings, Incentives, Conferences & Exhibitions) visitors. However, the authorities have started to take action to rejuvenate in order avoid the city's tourism industry declining. However, owing to the exponential growth in tourism, in particular, the increasing number of tourists from emerging economies, the number of first-time visitors was still growing until the coronavirus pandemic took hold in 2020.

Jost Krippendorf's *The Holiday Makers* (Krippendorf 1984) also discussed the issue of the local host population and the difference between what they expect and what they get from tourism. In line with the rapid growth in global tourism an increasing number of popular destinations have reached the critical consolidation stage including some of Europe's most visited cities: Venice, Barcelona, Amsterdam, and Lisbon. As discussed earlier, prior to the coronavirus pandemic, tourism had already reached unsustainable levels in many destinations. Regardless of the potential economic benefits, the negative impacts of overtourism on local residents were increasingly alienating host communities. However, owing to the increased number of travelers from the BRIC countries and other countries with emerging economies, it may be argued that fewer destinations are entering the stagnation stage than originally envisaged in Butler's tourism area lifecycle model.

It is evident that mature destinations that should have reached the stagnation stage or started to decline are those that are frequently faced with overtourism. The anticipated stagnation or decline has not happened as envisaged by Butler and Krippendorf. Instead, the number of tourists has continued to increase at a rapid rate driven by a growing world population, rising affluence, and global mass mobility. Newly affluent travelers from emerging markets are continuing to visit destinations on their bucket list that are already overcrowded, replacing those tourists who no longer find the destination attractive or satisfactory to visit.

However, it is clear that continuous investment in visitor-related infrastructure and management is required by the public and private sectors if destinations are to avoid overtourism in the future and in order to change local people's increasingly negative perception and experience of the tourism sector. Thus, there is an urgent need for destinations to consider how they may recover from the coronavirus post pandemic and regenerate in a more sustainable way that is socially inclusive and place local people's quality of life at the center. Tourism played a key role in economic recovery and growth post the 2008 global crisis and indeed has the potential to do the same post the coronavirus pandemic, but this time sustainability and resilience should be at the forefront.

Investment in tourism-related infrastructure is a joint responsibility between the public and private sectors. Investment in alternative product development and new visitor itineraries in mature destinations can be a successful way to disperse visitor flows and spread the benefits of tourism across a wider geographical area. This route is currently being pursued by Wonderful Copenhagen as a means to avoid overtourism from occurring in the most frequently visited parts of the city center (10xCopenhagen 2020).

Furthermore, investment in smart city technologies and artificial intelligence to monitor congestion and traffic flows can help local authorities and DMOs to better manage visitor flows and avoid overcrowding during peak times by controlling these electronically. Such technologies are already successfully used by theme parks who are continually investing in crowd control in order to accommodate growth and increase visitor spend, while at the same time implementing yield management and improving infrastructure capacity. In essence, the major theme parks have an effective crowd management plan in place at all times to ensure a high-quality visitor experience resulting in high spends and less crowding, something DMOs can learn from. The coronavirus pandemic and the sharp reduction in tourism demand has provided destinations with an opportunity to prepare for a more sustainable recovery and put plans in place aimed at managing future growth.

## Key Takeaways

1. Mature destinations that should have reached the stagnation stage in the lifecycle or even experienced a decline in visitation have frequently been faced with overtourism due to the rapid growth in international tourism, especially from emerging economies.

2. Investment in tourism-related infrastructure and smart technologies is required on an ongoing basis by the public and private sector to ensure destinations are able to plan for and accommodate future tourism growth.

# CHAPTER 6

# Measuring and Monitoring Destination Success to Avoid Overtourism

## Introduction

Traditionally, measuring the volume of tourists has been the key driver and indicator of growth and in turn destination success. However, this method falls short in a number of ways as it does not necessarily take into account the expenditure and behavioral patterns of different types of visitors.

In order to tackle overtourism it is crucial for destinations to understand which visitors deliver the most added value economically and the least negative social and environmental impacts. For destinations wishing to manage tourism in a sustainable manner, this requires creating a sophisticated set of baseline performance indicators. In turn, these can be measured and monitored on a regular basis to provide an up-to-date evidence base to inform tourism policy and measures to address and mitigate overtourism.

## Measuring and Understanding Tourism Performance

The International Recommendations for Tourism Statistics (IRTS) (International Recommendations For Tourism Statistics 2008, 2008) defines a visitor as a traveler taking a trip to a main destination outside his/her usual environment, for less than a year, for any main purpose (business, leisure, or other personal purpose) other than to be employed in the country visited. A visitor is a tourist if his/her trip includes an overnight stay; otherwise, a visitor is classified as a same-day visitor or excursionist (also known as a daytripper).

Tourism can be divided into three separate categories:

- **Domestic tourism:** Comprising the activities of a resident visitor within the country of reference.
- **Inbound tourism:** Comprising the activities of a nonresident visitor within the country of reference.
- **Outbound tourism:** Comprising the activities of a resident visitor outside the country of reference.

In order to measure the flow of visitors, both arrivals and nights are used to assess the number and length of stay of visitors. As far as overnight tourism is concerned, accommodation statistics are an important statistical source of information on domestic and inbound visitors.

The recent media coverage of the overtourism phenomenon does not tend to make a distinction between tourists and visitors even though the evidence indicates that daytrippers are one of the key drivers of overtourism. Daytrippers often arrive in large groups either on a coach or cruise ship and can be difficult for destinations to measure and manage. For example, a day visitor arriving by coach or cruise ship is likely to spend much less in the destination than someone who stays overnight in a hotel and eats all their meals in local restaurants. Furthermore, large groups arriving and departing at the same time (typically morning and late afternoon) tend to cause more congestion at key sites.

The highly regarded tourism expert Victor Middleton famously said: "You cannot manage what you cannot measure" (Tourism Society 2020). He went on to identify seven core tourism terms that are fundamental to any destination as well as understanding what to manage and measure:

1. Tourism
2. Visitors (tourists, same day visitors, leisure day visits)
3. Tourism industries
4. Visitor economy
5. Visitor destination/tourism destination
6. Destination management
7. Public realm

In order for destinations to avoid overtourism reoccurring in the future or occurring in the first place, there is a need for a paradigm shift toward measuring value creation rather than volume as the key measure of success in order to address any potential negative impacts and work toward the long-term sustainability of destinations. In its latest publication Tourism Trends and Policies 2020, the OECD recommends that destinations "ensure access to comparable and timely data to inform decision making and better plan for the type and scale of tourism growth appropriate for individual destinations" (OECD Tourism Trends and Policies 2020 | en | OECD 2020). Such actions will also help make destinations more resilient in the future.

Timely and regular tourism data collection and analytics are key to understanding and preventing overtourism. Understanding visitors and their behaviors to ensure maximum value creation at the destination level is essential and this typically involves improving data analysis to take into account environmental and sustainability criteria. Although, most countries collect regular and timely data at the national and regional level, high-quality data is often lacking at the local level, especially outside the key cities where there is a limited number of registered accommodation establishments. This can be an issue particularly at natural hot spots that fall victim to overtourism and are located in relatively remote areas.

The majority of destinations collect data on visitor arrivals, visitor nights, jobs, and the economic contribution of tourism. Many destinations also regularly conduct visitor satisfaction surveys that can be used to provide early warning signals that a destination is reaching saturation point leading to a deterioration in the visitor experience. Dr. Gang Li, Professor of Tourism and Economics at University of Surrey, UK, recently highlighted the importance of understanding visitor satisfaction: "nobody is really measuring tourist happiness and the impact of tourism on wellbeing, yet these are the insights that would help hospitality businesses and destinations to perform better in the future." At Ecole Hotelier Lausanne's third Annual Hospitality Finance and Economics Research Conference, Dr. Gang Li pointed out that many tourists pursue happiness on their travels and thus this should be an important measure used to inform the future of tourism. This is important for several reasons including that satisfied visitors (Tourism satisfaction: importance, measurability, and impacts—Insights 2020):

- Tend to stay longer, spend more, and are more likely to revisit.
- Are more likely to promote the destination via word of mouth, social media, and online reviews thereby enhancing the destination's competitiveness.
- Are likely to bring friends and family on any subsequent visit.
- Find that holiday satisfaction has a positive impact on their overall quality of life.

Dr. Gang Li's research and methods of evaluating tourist experiences in South Africa concluded the following:

- High-cost experiences generally equal less happiness because the product does not seem to be worth the cost.
- High-quality experiences make people happy and often feature interactive and interpersonal experiences, sensory experiences and humorous, fun or exciting activities, and people such as staff and guides.
- Any disagreement or complaint has a negative overall impact.
- Good tourism experiences create wellbeing that spills over into other areas of life. Therefore, it is not unfair to market tourism as something that changes and shapes one's life, but the experience has to live up to expectations (Tourism satisfaction: importance, measurability and impacts—Insights 2020).

The previous points highlight the importance of conducting visitor satisfaction surveys soon after the visit (e.g., exit surveys at the point of departure) so that an understanding of expectation versus reality can be reached. Identifying what makes a positive visitor experience at the destination level as well as what makes a bad experience will enable destination managers to focus on enhancing the aspects of the experience that have the most significant impact on visitor satisfaction levels.

Smart cities are making it possible to gather data about where people are, what they are doing and increasing services in response to peaks and troughs in demand using smartphone technology for example to measure congestion. This can help create a better balance between local resident movements and tourist flows in busy cities. Big data analysis can be particularly useful when it comes to understanding tourist flows generated by daytrippers by combining different sources of information such as mobile phone, Wi-Fi, and credit card activity data to understand volume and movement patterns and in turn generate real-time heat maps. Subsequently, these can be used to instantly promote alternative less crowded sites. For example, it is indicated on the website of the Palace of Versailles that during peak hours visitors should expect wait times of between an hour and 90 minutes. The website suggests visiting the palace during the off-peak times such as the afternoon to reduce waiting time. Furthermore, the ticketing system allows visitors to skip the queue by purchasing a more expensive ticket (Pechlaner, Innerhofer and Erschbamer 2020).

As stated previously, tourism data is usually collected at the national and regional level, but it can be hard to breakdown and analyze at the local level. There is a need for sufficient data, in particular at the regional and local level, to understand tourism's full impact and to inform how the tourism sector should evolve and grow in the future at the destination level. It is generally recognized that there is a lack of agreed upon common indicators and monitoring tools available to destinations and DMOs to enable them to assess whether they are at risk of overtourism. As a first step toward monitoring a destination's performance vis-à-vis overtourism occurring, DMOs should develop a bespoke checklist to include all or some of the indicators shown in Table 6.1. This should enable DMOs to build a reliable evidence base to guide decision making and introduce appropriate measures as and when necessary. Once a bespoke set of indicators have been developed and agreed upon at the destination level these can be used to monitor the performance of the tourism industry and in turn deliver more effective destination management.

Ideally, such a checklist should be developed into a widely shared and accessible destination dashboard illustrating the tourism industry's relative performance against the agreed indicators. Tourism Australia has an excellent dashboard, albeit not related to overtourism it could be used

*Table 6.1  Destination overtourism monitoring checklist*

| Key Indicators | 1999 | 2009 | 2015 | 2016 | 2017 | 2018 | 2019 | CAGR1 (1999 to 2019) | CAGR (2016 to 2019) |
|---|---|---|---|---|---|---|---|---|---|
| Destination area (km²) | | | | | | | | | |
| Resident Population | | | | | | | | | |
| Airport distance (km) | | | | | | | | | |
| Airport destinations served | | | | | | | | | |
| Annual and monthly air passenger movements (000s) | | | | | | | | | |
| Cruise port distance (km) | | | | | | | | | |
| Annual and monthly cruise ship calls | | | | | | | | | |
| Annual and monthly cruise passengers | | | | | | | | | |
| Annual and monthly tourists Arrivals | | | | | | | | | |
| Annual and monthly overnight Stays in Registered Accommodation | | | | | | | | | |

¹Compound annual growth rate percent

Table 6.1 Continued

| Key Indicators | 1999 | 2009 | 2015 | 2016 | 2017 | 2018 | 2019 | CAGR1 (1999 to 2019) | CAGR (2016 to 2019) |
|---|---|---|---|---|---|---|---|---|---|
| Supply of Registered Accommodation (Rooms and/or Beds) | | | | | | | | | |
| Supply of Airbnb/Booking.com units | | | | | | | | | |
| Annual and monthly accommodation occupancy statistics | | | | | | | | | |
| Annual and monthly visitors to top five attractions | | | | | | | | | |
| Tourism's share of GDP/GVA | | | | | | | | | |
| Visitor satisfaction surveys | | | | | | | | | |
| Resident sentiment surveys | | | | | | | | | |
| Social media monitoring including negative reviews | | | | | | | | | |

as an inspiration. In most destinations DMOs are ideally placed to take on this responsibility. The checklist and an associated user-friendly dashboard should be updated at least on an annual basis in order to act as a tool for DMOs and destination managers to monitor any potential risk of overtourism. This will provide DMOs with an opportunity to introduce mitigating measures as required when warning signals are raised. The checklist and associated data can be used to calculate the ratio of tourists and daytrippers to local residents in order to identify if there are signs of the local host population becoming marginalized. Regular monitoring of social media, such as negative reviews on TripAdvisor, together with conducting regular visitor surveys will help to flag any potential deterioration in the quality of the visitor experience as well as any degradation of the destination's image.

Furthermore, the rapid growth in sharing economy platforms such as Airbnb means that this type of overnight stay is frequently not captured in the tourism statistics collected making it difficult to assess the true impact. The popularity of staying in short-term rentals has grown rapidly in recent years and has clearly filled a gap in the market in terms of the type of accommodation visitors are seeking. Visit Denmark has reached a data sharing agreement with Airbnb so that estimates can be made with regard to the number of bednights generated by sharing economy platforms which is considered a key step forward. As described earlier, Airbnb has vowed to collaborate with DMOs to prevent overtourism from reoccurring in the future (Airbnb partners with Visit Denmark 2017).

It is critical to collect regular and consistent time-series data so that destination performance and development can be measured on an ongoing basis as well as over time in order to truly understand and monitor emerging trends and their impacts of the tourism sector. The data should be readily available and shared online via a dashboard for industry stakeholders, the local community, and residents as well as for others to see. The use of a checklist such as the one shown in Table 6.1 goes a long way toward early detection of possible signs of overtourism. However, it is clear that going forward there needs to be much more emphasis on how the tourism industry can become more sustainable and respond to growing consumer awareness and concerns. As discussed, the vast majority of travel and tourism companies are lagging behind in this regard and therefore should be encouraged to be accountable in terms of the triple bottom line that measures the economic, social, and environmental costs of a business. According to the Travel Foundation:

> this will enable the tourism industry to look at opportunities to minimise the risks and costs of continuous tourism growth. Ideally, destinations need to be able to measure and manage the cost of each tourist in order to assess which segments provide the most benefits at local level. This will require systems that calculate the costs of tourism development on local economies. Without measuring the costs of tourism, it is virtually impossible to manage a destination effectively. Those costs include the infrastructure required to transport, feed and house, provide energy and water, and manage waste and wastewater for the growing number of visitors and tourism sector workers at the destination level. Local tourism sector burdens such as air pollution and water scarcity are often invisible and ignore the management burden and costs at the local destination level (Destinations at Risk: The Invisible Burden of Tourism—Travel Foundation 2019).

This is a great mid- to long-term aspiration, but it will require significant effort to develop across all destinations. Currently, there is a general disconnect between the national, regional, and local destination level in the tourism sector in most countries. This disconnect makes effective destination management extremely challenging as regional and local destinations tend to compete against each other rather than collaborate. At the same time, tourism-related data and statistics tend to be collected mainly at the national and regional level, which means that it can be difficult to measure the impact of tourism at the local level where the actual impact, positive or negative, occurs and in turn make evidence-based decisions. Thus, there is a need to streamline data collection including at the local level so that the impact of tourism is measured where it occurs especially in tourism hotspots. In many countries DMOs vary significantly in terms of size, remit, funding, and organizational set up, which means they sometimes overlap geographically as well as across administrative levels.

Historically, destinations have tended to use a linear model to measure and forecast economic value when in reality it is more likely that value will develop in a bell curve—more tourists do not necessarily equate to higher spends. According to Doug Lansky this is often explained by the fact that the most influential stakeholders at the destination level tend to operate according to a linear business model; for example, airlines, cruise lines, hotels, and restaurants, which is not necessarily compatible with a more selective approach that may be required to attract low-volume and high-value tourists in order to avoid overtourism (Lansky 2020). Measuring the environmental and especially social impacts of the tourism industry has been lacking to date. Although, a number of destinations including Barcelona and Copenhagen have started to conduct regular surveys with local residents in order to better understand and monitor the impact of the tourism sector on local residents.

There is a need for destinations to take a long-term strategic view and make data-driven decisions. The coronavirus pandemic was a good time for destinations to review the traditional volume-centric business model and shift the focus toward the visitors that can deliver the best value in the long term. During the pandemic, destinations were faced with substantially reduced demand and prepared themselves for lengthy disruption as the crisis developed and retreated at a different pace across the world. It appears likely that the initial policy focus, for the vast majority of destinations, post pandemic will be on returning to "business as usual" rather than a major change in the approach to managing tourism. However, for the long term, following the early recovery period, it will be crucial to shift the emphasis toward managing destinations in a more sustainable manner. This will likely mean adopting a more selective approach to visitor segmentation in order to distribute the benefits created by tourism better throughout society to ensure that local people are the primary beneficiaries.

## Key Takeaways

- Traditionally success of the tourism sector has been based on growth in volume and to a lesser extent economic contribution.

- There is a need for a paradigm shift toward understanding which visitor segments add the most value/benefit at the local destination level and have the least negative environmental and social impact.
- Regular monitoring and analysis of key baseline indicators is required to understand tourism flows and impacts in order to avoid overtourism.
- Developing a bespoke destination checklist and dashboard will enable destinations and DMOs to take appropriate measures to address and mitigate overtourism in order to manage destinations effectively.

# CHAPTER 7

# The Role of Effective Destination Management in Managing Tourism

## Introduction

This chapter explores the role of effective destination management in managing tourism for long-term success and sustainability. It argues how overtourism may be reversed or avoided through effective destination management. Typically, this involves engaging with key industry stakeholders and local residents as well as handling visitor flows more efficiently throughout the day or the year. This in turn can help preserve the local residents' quality of life while at the same time delivering a high-quality experience for visitors.

In order to deliver positive tourism growth in the future, destinations and DMOs need to prepare for recovery post the coronavirus pandemic by focusing on all three pillars of sustainability in order to manage tourism destinations in a responsible manner. This requires an appropriately structured and funded DMO.

## Destination Management Organization (DMO) Structure

The UNWTO defines a DMO as a "leading organisational entity which may encompass various authorities, stakeholders and professionals and facilitates partnerships toward a collective destination vision" (A Practical Guide to Tourism Destination Management | UNWTO 2018). DMOs tend to vary significantly in terms of their governance, organizational structure, remit, and funding model. Some are a single public authority while many are based on a public–private partnership model and others are purely private entities. Furthermore, DMOs can operate at local, regional, or national level, and some destinations do not have a DMO. DMOs that rely on funding by key private sector stakeholders can face a major dilemma when trying to address overtourism, especially if that involves imposing regulations and restrictions on private sector operators in order to limit or reduce visitation from certain segments including coach groups or cruise passengers.

According to the UNWTO: "The DMO emerges as a key player in the development and management of tourism at the destination level, although its mandate and scope of action will be determined by its context, maturity of the destination, resources and other factors" (A Practical Guide to Tourism Destination Management | UNWTO 2018). In summary DMOs are as diverse as destinations. However, traditionally, the primary purpose of DMOs has been destination marketing and promotion. As destinations have evolved and the tourism sector has grown the remit and responsibilities of DMOs have become increasingly broad, but often with limited additional funding and decision-making power.

DMOs are frequently having to take on the responsibility as a mediator between the public and private sectors as well as the local host population, especially when it comes to dealing with overtourism. In recent years, it has become increasingly clear that DMOs need to collaborate more widely and influence a wider and more complex range of stakeholders in order to be successful. Tourism can no longer exist in isolation from the wider local socioeconomic and environmental context, but must form an integral of any long-term plans. A DMO must achieve strategic buy-in from all key stakeholders as well as the local host population and politicians, which requires an appropriate governance model.

The UNWTO considers that effectively managed and coordinated destinations are more likely to have a strong evidence base enabling them to stay on top of trends. This allows them to develop innovative products in order to deliver a high-quality visitor experience and remain competitive (A Practical Guide to Tourism Destination Management | UNWTO 2018). Given the inherent complexity of the tourism industry, some of the key roles and responsibilities of a successful DMO should include some or all of the following:

- **Purpose:** To deliver maximum benefit to the local host population based on flexible long-term strategy for the tourism sector. This should be founded on the three pillars of sustainability supported by an appropriate action and implementation plan.
- **Collaboration and partnerships:** Engage effective with key industry stakeholders, public sector, politicians, the local community and residents to build consensus and agree shared strategic goals and outcomes.
- **Communication and mediation:** Act as an interface between the public sector, key industry stakeholders, local community, residents, and visitors to minimize any friction and encourage tourism sector buy-in.
- **Tourism development:** Collaborate with public sector and tourism industry businesses to drive innovation, tourism product development, and sustainability. Support entrepreneurs, micros, and SMEs as these are key to local value creation and enhancing the tourism multiplier effect.
- **Monitoring:** Research and analysis to measure the performance of the tourism sector against an agreed set of key indicators on a regular and timely basis. Performance measurement is a crucial tool with regard to short-, medium- and long-term planning to avoid overtourism and ensure that tourism delivers maximum local benefits as well as contribute toward a balanced economy.
- **Crisis management:** Emergency preparedness and ability to act promptly during any crisis; the coronavirus pandemic being a case in point.
- **Marketing and promotion:** Maintain the destination's brand and reputation as well as attracting those visitors likely to generate the maximum local benefits at minimum social and environmental costs. Furthermore, there is scope to use

instant advertising and promotion to divert visitors away from key sites during peak periods of demand to avoid congestion.

- **Funding and investment:** In visitor-related infrastructure to ensure that the destination remains competitive and avoids overtourism due to congestion and overcrowding (A Practical Guide to Tourism Destination Management | UNWTO 2018).

## Effective Destination Management Principles

From the early days of mass tourism, it has been recognized that the pressures caused by tourism can damage the places that tourists travel to visit in the first place. Today tourism is seen as a right by many, and economic advances and commercial opportunities have fueled the rapid growth in international tourism owing to global mass mobility. Thus, the challenge for today's destination management professionals is to manage the sector effectively and responsibly to avoid overtourism caused by congestion and overcrowding from reoccurring. Many destinations could learn how to better manage visitor flows from major theme park operators such as Disney. Not only are their parks pristine and well maintained, but they excel at crowd management in order to create the best possible visitor experience and maximize spend, which in turn means more on the bottom line.

While many destinations are successful at building new museums, establishing nature reserves and so forth, unfortunately, many fail to get the basics such as transport, parking, signposting, and other visitor-related infrastructure right. This is because the responsibility for these tend to rest with the government or local authority (rather than the DMO) who often lack an in-depth knowledge of the travel and tourism sector. Undoubtedly, this infrastructure forms a key part of creating an authentic and high-quality satisfying visitor experience, so if the infrastructure is not fit for purpose, it is unlikely that a visitor will return. In the worst-case scenario, they will probably share their bad experience instantly across social media with their friends and peers. Investing in the basic tourism infrastructure should be common sense for most destinations be they small remote islands or large iconic destinations such as Venice. One of the key challenges is that most destinations are led by politicians who prefer large flagship projects over

implementing an efficient and visitor-friendly parking system or introducing controversial tourism tax/levy to fund investment. A holistic approach
to destination management is required in order to avoid overcrowding and
increasing visitor numbers from becoming a burden for the destination, its
stakeholders, residents, and local community.

Tourism is a key economic driver in many destinations around the
world, but it needs to be taken seriously at all levels of government in
order to be sustainable and achieve the desired economic outcomes. This
also means taking environmental and social impacts into account. Many
governments and local authorities underestimate and fail to recognize
tourism as an industry owing to its highly fragmented nature, which in
turn makes it a challenge to manage and regulate.

Putting in place an appropriate regulatory and legislative framework to avoid overtourism requires strong leadership, collaboration, and
building consensus among key industry stakeholders and with the local
community and residents at the destination level. This can be difficult
to achieve for a DMO without an appropriate governance model. Many
politicians do not fully understand the dynamics of the tourism sector
and the concept that more visitors do not necessarily equate to a higher
economic contribution and may indeed result in higher social and environmental costs. The question is, who is in charge of protecting destinations especially at the local level where resources are often lacking?

With regard to governance, it is useful to adopt a model that considers
a "whole-of-destination" approach, which may take the form of a Tourism
Destination Task Force or Steering Group. Ideally, this should comprise
key public and private sector stakeholders as well as community representatives who meet on a regular basis to discuss tourism issues, challenges,
and solutions and ultimately achieve a joined-up approach. One of the
advantages of such a governance model is that it facilitates that tourism
becomes embedded and prioritized with other economic develop activities and planning considerations without getting lost within the wider
destination. Such a model also enables a DMO to provide strategic advice
and guidance on tourism product and infrastructure development as well
investment requirements.

Currently, building a resilient and sustainable tourism sector requires
a shift toward maximizing the economic benefits through attracting the

right kind of visitor while at the same time seeking to minimize any negative environmental and social impacts. This involves a shift away from marketing and promotion toward integrating tourism with the destination's wider land-use planning, housing, retail, and mobility strategies. Amsterdam, Barcelona, Copenhagen, Lisbon, and Paris have taken steps in the right direction as highlighted throughout this book.

According to *The World*, Amsterdam adopted Kate Raworth's Donut economic model as part of its coronavirus recovery plan for people and the planet (Raworth 2020). A key element of donut economic thinking is no longer using GDP/GVA as a proxy for society's success. Post pandemic, Amsterdam is not looking to instantly replace the 20 million annual visitors, but rather seeking to make the city healthy and resilient by focusing on affordable housing and jobs for the community.

Traditional DMOs with a marketing and promotion focus are not set up nor do they have sufficient funding to take on a wider leadership remit as well as the responsibility for monitoring and regulating the tourism industry. However, overcoming overtourism requires governments and local authorities to make bold decisions and take actions (often regulatory) that are not always going to be popular with all stakeholders. An example of such bold action is the Seychelles whose tourism minister announced a two-year ban on cruise ships in May 2020 (Marcus 2020). Officially, this was a move to minimize any chance of a second wave of coronavirus infections, but it could also be seen as a more strategic move to minimize the future number of visitors and in turn potentially avoid overtourism. Similarly, Barcelona City Council recognizes that it has limited influence over Barcelona Port, which makes it difficult to agree a joint strategy on how to tackle overtourism caused by daytrippers including cruise passengers. To put this into context, in 1990 Barcelona received just 115,000 cruise passengers, but by 2019 this had increased to 2.9 million making Barcelona Europe's busiest cruise port and the fourth busiest in the world. On 139 days of the year the number of cruise passengers visiting the city exceeds 10,000 with the busiest day of the week being Friday. Hence, Barcelona Port is probably the most influential stakeholder when it comes to managing the volume of daytrippers visiting the city (Burgen 2019).

It is evident that effective destination management and good governance is required in terms of planning and managing the complex infrastructure requirements for tourists in order to accommodate future long-term growth in visitor numbers. An effective destination management approach needs to take into account seasonality patterns including peak periods and how these can be managed through dispersal of visitor flows to other periods of the year or alternative geographical locations to avoid congestion. However, investment in new/or overloaded infrastructure and tourism products may be required to achieve such diversification and de-seasonalization. This requires a move away from the traditional marketing and promotion-focused DMOs toward managing visitors effectively. Many DMOs are partially or fully funded by private sector stakeholders who may not have the same goals as the destination overall, for example the primary objectives of airports and cruise ports will be to maximize the number of passengers at all times, which may contradict a destination's desire to reduce visitor flows at certain peak times. The voice of the local host population is often not heard, which can lead to discontent when visitor numbers increase rapidly, and the destination approaches saturation point or its carrying capacity.

## Stakeholder Influence and Engagement

In order for a destination or DMO to engage effectively with stakeholders, it is critical to understand the level of influence the various identified stakeholders have. The tourism sector carries a high reputational risk for politicians and governments if tourism goes wrong. This has been shown during the coronavirus pandemic, which has demonstrated that both too much and too little tourism are equally undesirable. It is therefore essential for DMOs to engage effectively with the most influential stakeholders in order to build consensus and collaborate to achieve the desired destination goals and outcomes for the long term.

Many DMOs fail to understand who the most influential stakeholders are—most will argue that it is the government, but that is not necessarily always the case.

## Stakeholder Influence Mapping

Whenever working on a strategic project that requires stakeholder buy-in in order to implement the identified actions, the starting point is usually a destination capsule situation analysis, which will include a stakeholder mapping exercise to identify who the most influential stakeholders are. In the case of Iceland, the conclusion was that the most influential stakeholder was Icelandair Group, which was not very popular with the public sector. However, at the end of the strategy process Icelandair Group did not buy into the strategy and commissioned a separate piece of work, which meant that the strategy recommendations were never implemented in full.

A useful tool is to conduct a simple stakeholder mapping exercise aligned to the destination's strategic goals in order to identify the most influential stakeholders including those that may need to be convinced and influenced to ensure the destination's long-term success. Table 7.1 is an example of a stakeholder mapping exercise completed as part of a *Long-term Strategy for the Icelandic Tourism Industry* in 2011 to 2012 (i.e., prior to the aforementioned rapid growth resulting in overtourism in specific places at certain times of the year).

On the top line the table shows the selected indicators against which each key stakeholder was assessed with each identified stakeholder/stakeholder groups shown down the side. A simple scoring method was used with one dot equating to little influence and three dots implying a high degree of influence. The stakeholder mapping exercise was completed in close collaboration with the client Promote Iceland and showed the level of influence of various tourism industry stakeholders in Iceland, based on their ability to control and influence the tourism strategy objectives as well as their influence on policy, budget, and access to funding.

It is clear from Table 7.1 and the accompanying scores that there were a number of very influential large stakeholders in Iceland at the time (namely, Icelandair Group, the Ministry of Industries and Innovation, Visit Reykjavík, and the Icelandic Tourist Board) who were dominating the voice of the tourism industry. It was also evident that the smaller industry stakeholders, who are often private sector micro- or SME businesses, tended to have much less influence, even though they are crucially important in terms of the provision and delivery of services to visitors. It is also worth noting that there were no cruise industry or local community representatives included as stakeholders at the time, even though there was a certain level of awareness that local residents, especially in Reykjavík and the south, had concerns about the rapid growth in tourism.

It was evident that the Icelandic tourism industry was made up of a few large dominant players as well as a plethora of innovative entrepreneurial micros and SMEs offering a huge range of activities and products. The micros and SMEs formed an important part of the supply chain and had a crucial role to play in supporting livelihoods through job creation especially in the more rural and remote areas. At the time there was no consensus nor shared goals, which resulted in lack of coherence among stakeholders and prevented them from working in a collaborative manner in order to achieve consensus. As mentioned, at the time there were voices of concern that the tourism industry was growing too rapidly and that it was too much for the small local resident population to cope with. Nonetheless, possibly due to lack consensus among the industry stakeholders, the number of tourists to Iceland increased at an almost exponential rate largely driven by increased airlift and destination reach by Icelandair as well as a number of low-cost carriers combined with growth in cruise ship calls and passengers. At the time it was recommended that in the future tourism in Iceland needed to be developed in a manner that was appropriate to the scale and size of the country and its small population. The focus needed to be on value, economic growth, and profitability rather than purely volume.

Coincidentally, the 2012 strategy recommendations included capping the number of annual visitors at one million, limiting the size and number of cruise ships and introducing a conservation fee to pay for tourism-related infrastructure development outside the heavily visited Golden Circle to encourage wider dispersal of tourist flows across the island. If these recommendations had been implemented at the time, Iceland would probably not have faced overtourism to the extent it has.

The *2012 Long-term strategy for the Icelandic tourism industry* considered that with gradual growth in volume, it would be possible to reach one million tourists per annum in five years and around 1.5 million by 2030 (Long-term strategy for the Iceland tourism industry 2012). At the time, Iceland knew where it was at, but not where it wanted to be in 2030? It was recommended that sustainability and economic growth should be at the core of the future of tourism in Iceland and many stakeholders agreed. But, unfortunately, there was no clear consensus owing to the previously mentioned lack of strategic stakeholder alignment. However, there was a

Table 7.1 Stakeholder influence mapping Iceland

| Areas of influence Stakeholder | Policy | Funding and Budget | Marketing and Promotion | Tourism Services and Infrastructure | Nature and Environment | Standards and Quality | Access and Seasonality | Overall Score |
|---|---|---|---|---|---|---|---|---|
| Icelandair Group | •• | ••• | ••• | ••• | •• | •• | ••• | 18 |
| Ministry of Industries and Innovation | ••• | ••• | •• | •• | •• | ••• | •• | 17 |
| Visit Reykjavik | •• | ••• | •• | ••• | •• | •• | •• | 16 |
| Icelandic Tourist Board | •• | •• | •• | •• | •• | ••• | •• | 15 |
| Ministry for Environment and Natural Resources | ••• | •• | • | ••• | ••• | •• | • | 15 |
| Promote Iceland | •• | ••• | ••• | •• | • | • | •• | 14 |
| Meet in Reykjavik | • | ••• | •• | •• | •• | •• | •• | 14 |
| Isavia | •• | •• | • | ••• | • | •• | ••• | 14 |
| Icelandic Travel Industry Association | •• | • | • | ••• | •• | ••• | • | 13 |
| Innovation Center Iceland | •• | •• | • | •• | •• | •• | •• | 13 |

*Table 7.1 Continued*

| Areas of influence Stakeholder | Policy | Funding and Budget | Marketing and Promotion | Tourism Services and Infrastructure | Nature and Environment | Standards and Quality | Access and Seasonality | Overall Score |
|---|---|---|---|---|---|---|---|---|
| Incoming tour operators | • | • | • | ••• | •• | ••• | •• | 13 |
| Icelandic Farm Holidays Association | • | • | • | | ••• | | •• | 12 |
| Regional Tourist Boards | •• | • | •• | •• | •• | •• | • | 12 |
| Hotels and Restaurants | • | • | • | ••• | •• | ••• | • | 12 |
| SMEs/Entrepreneurs | • | • | • | ••• | •• | ••• | • | 12 |
| Harpa | • | • | •• | •• | • | • | •• | 10 |
| Icelandic Equestrian Association | • | •• | • | | •• | •• | • | 10 |
| Icelandic Tourism Research Center | •• | • | • | •• | • | • | • | 9 |

lot of public interest in tourism locally at the time and during a public consultation exercise tourism came out as the top topic. In retrospect, it is interesting to note that Iceland reached around 2.3 million tourist arrivals in 2018 representing an average annual growth rate of 23.8 percent over five years. Although, this subsequently dropped back to around two million in 2019, it illustrates how lack of stakeholder alignment and consensus can be a major factor in overtourism, especially when the concerns of the local resident population are largely ignored. Fortunately, for Iceland the new 12-year National Infrastructure Plan introduced in 2018 appears to take a long-term view on infrastructure development at public sites of natural and cultural heritage under pressure from tourism owing to the rapid growth of the sector since 2010. This plan supplemented by a dispersal strategy that seeks to distribute visitors more widely across Iceland and away from the key hot spots in the south. Hopefully, this is not too little or too late for Iceland.

## Shift DMO Focus Toward Effective Management of Tourism Sector

As destinations attract a growing number of visitors and get closer to reaching saturation point or their carrying capacity, the need for destination marketing and promotion becomes less important. At the same time effective management of wider destination issues becomes increasingly important in order to mitigate and avoid overtourism. According to the Travel Foundation there is a growing need for targeted interventions to protect tourism assets worldwide with a focus on the root causes of overtourism. As described earlier in this chapter, this will require more DMOs to move away from purely marketing and promoting the destination to managing the tourism sector for maximum local benefit.

When Barcelona's tourism department published its Barcelona Tourism for 2020 in March 2017 (Barcelona Tourism for 2020—A collective strategy for sustainable tourism 2020), there were no signs of a global pandemic that would bring tourism to a virtual standstill at the beginning of 2020, rather the city was faced with how to manage a destination that had become a victim of its own success with a sustained increase in visitors having transformed the city's urban fabric, mobility, and economic activities as well as the daily life of many neighborhoods. Barcelona's territorial features make it a small city in geographical terms (101km$^2$) with a high population density of 15,887 residents per km$^2$. With visitors tending to concentrate in key iconic locations it is not a surprise that rapid growth in visitor numbers led to congestion and overtourism in certain public spaces. Thus, the strategy set out to challenge: "a change from managing tourism in the city to managing the tourist city, making it compatible with other needs of a multiple, complex and heterogeneous city such as Barcelona" (Barcelona Tourism for 2020—A collective strategy for sustainable tourism 2020). It went beyond traditional tourism strategies that seek to promote a destination in order to attract an increasing number of visitors to switching the focus to governance and management of congested areas. Unusually, for a tourism strategy and critically, the strategy development process included consulting with over 200 representatives from local resident associations, companies, trade unions, cultural and social organizations who all became part of the new debate and vision for tourism in Barcelona. The plan looked at tourism's potential for local development and considered how this could be integrated with territorial business and social initiatives in order to stimulate the multiplier effect from tourism and adding value at local level. Sustainability was considered essential to ensure that tourism remains an innovative and enriching activity for the City of Barcelona. However, the absence of tourists owing to the coronavirus pandemic means that the Barcelona Tourist Board had to re-evaluate its priorities toward a more moderate way of tourism initially targeting the domestic market and neighboring international markets as well as focusing more on specific sectors.

The WTTC recognizes that there are no simple solutions to overtourism nor a one-size-fits-all model. However, it lists the following as possible solutions to overtourism in the short-, medium- and long-term (McKinsey & Company 2017):

1. Smooth visitors over time
2. Spread visitors across sites
3. Adjust pricing to balance supply and demand
4. Regulate accommodation supply
5. Limit access and activities

The previously mentioned solutions have been discussed and high-lighted with case studies throughout this book and it appears that a combination of such measures can help reduce the likelihood of overtourism reoccurring in the future. However, perhaps equally important for DMOs, is the need to communicate and engage with key industry stake-holders as well as the local host population and community to ensure that the tourism sector delivers maximum benefits and contributes toward a balanced economy.

## Using the Coronavirus Pandemic Crisis Management to Address Overtourism

The coronavirus pandemic is providing destinations previously suffering from overtourism with a once-in-a-lifetime opportunity to reset and refo-cus their tourism sector ensuring that sustainability and community are at the core going forward.

A golden rule in any crisis is to start planning for recovery as soon as that crisis starts. Winston Churchill famously said: "Never let a crisis go to waste." The coronavirus pandemic has put the tourism industry into perspective and never has international cooperation and responsi-ble leadership been more important. The UNWTO believes that tourism will play an important role during the recovery phase when it eventually comes. The coronavirus crisis made it clear that the tourism value chain touches upon every part of society. This makes tourism uniquely placed to promote solidarity, collaboration, and concrete action across borders during challenging times and also ideally positioned to once again drive future recovery.

The following crisis recovery destination management checklist can act as a useful tool for DMOs looking to ensure that their destination emerges stronger and more resilient post the coronavirus pandemic. It includes three key phases (Hindle 2020):

**1. Prerecovery phase:**
- Continue communication with key stakeholders and visitor audiences—online briefings—keep talking

- Innovate with training and ideas to prepare for recovery
- Make new connections
- Change broadcast focus to welcoming visitors back when possible
- Consider long-leads
- Amplify local voices and encourage storytelling
- Fight fear with facts

**2. Emerging recovery phase:**
- Target those most likely to travel and visit
- Domestic audiences (staycation)
- Neighboring audiences (those who already know or are familiar with destination are most likely to return first)
- Repeat visitors
- Resilient visitors (special interest niche dedicated travelers)

**3. Full recovery and regeneration phase:**
- DMOs that spend time planning destination management recovery rather than focusing on marketing and promotion strategies in isolation will be in a position to deliver genuine long-term results at local level.

DMOs will need to consider what is travel likely to look like during the recovery phase and post the coronavirus pandemic? A CNN Travel article dated 30 March 2020 highlighted that people are still going to want to travel but may be more cautious in their choices and wishing to be reassured that traveling is safe. Cheaper prices are almost inevitable during the early stages of recovery. The cruise sector is particularly adversely affected, and it is likely to be very difficult to attract new customers even with heavily discounted prices owing to the high infection rates recorded on cruise ships. Hygiene and cleanliness have become crucial issues that will need to be addressed by operators across the travel and tourism industry (Hunter 2020).

Increased focus on sustainability is likely to be one of the positive outcomes of the coronavirus crisis. Prior to the pandemic overtourism, sustainable travel and the environment were among the most talked about topics facing the industry. The travel and tourism industry now has the opportunity to recover and regenerate in a much more responsible and ethical way and respond to consumers' growing concern with sustainability, especially in terms of climate change and social inclusivity.

## Key Takeaways

- The vast majority of DMOs were originally set up to market and promote destinations. With rapid growth in tourism there is a need to shift the emphasis toward managing wider destination issues in order to avoid overtourism. The coronavirus pandemic has provided destinations with an opportunity to reconsider the future of tourism.
- Effective stakeholder influencing and engagement with the public sector, key industry stakeholders, the local community, and residents are critical in order to achieve consensus and reach the destination's desired long-term strategic goals and outcomes.
- A DMO needs to be structured to organize the destination for success supported by a flexible and adaptable strategy and action plan. This requires an appropriate governance model so that tourism becomes an integrated part of the wider destination's economic and planning framework.
- DMOs need to work to ensure that maximum long-term local benefits are derived from tourism. This requires focusing on all three pillars of sustainability, but more than ever before the social and environmental aspects.

# CHAPTER 8

# Preserving the Quality of Life of the Local Community and Residents

## Introduction

It is paramount that DMOs take into account the local host community and residents as they should be the main beneficiaries of any successful tourism sector. As such the preservation or enhancement of their quality of life should be a major consideration when managing the destination. However, until recently, the voice of the local host population has often been ignored by DMOs.

## DMO Engagement With Local Host Community and Residents

The local host community and residents are the main beneficiaries and users of local infrastructure and facilities, some of which may not be viable without tourist flows. However, it can be difficult for DMOs to consult and engage effectively with the local host community, in particular, with local residents as this can be a highly fragmented stakeholder group of which many are not directly involved in the travel and tourism sector. Thus, engaging with the local host community and residents requires a participatory decision-making approach that considers both bottom-up and top-down solutions in order to the address multidimensional issue that overtourism is.

DMOs have an important role to play in promoting better understanding of the value of tourism to the local community and residents. In order to do so, it is critical to consult, engage, and collaborate with the local community in order to share the benefits of tourism and its success as well as discuss any negative impacts and perceptions. The tourism sector is labor intensive and has the potential to create local jobs and stimulate local enterprise, thereby creating inclusive growth that benefits the local community and fosters economic prosperity. The creation of social enterprises is a good way to ensure that the local community and residents remain the main beneficiaries of the tourism sector as illustrated by the Fogo Island Inn in Newfoundland, Canada.

At the destination level it is critical to consider and help facilitate the creation of quality jobs in order to ensure the local host population benefits from the development of the tourism sector. This has often been ignored by DMOs in the past partly due to their focus on marketing and promotion as well as being dependant on private-sector funding earmarked for this particular purpose. However, there is an increasing number of examples of destinations taking steps to engage more effectively with local residents on a proactive basis. For example, Barcelona carries out a periodic citizen perception survey that gathers the opinion of Barcelona's residents on tourism. The survey includes important district level information with a sufficiently large sample size to provide important data on neighborhoods with a larger tourist activity presence. In 2016, residents (90 percent of those surveyed) considered tourism to be beneficial to the city; however, this varied according to the area of the city. At the same time, 43 percent considered tourism to be reaching its limits in terms of Barcelona's capacity to accommodate and service visitors and cited it as the city's fourth biggest problem (Barcelona Tourism for 2020—A collective strategy for sustainable tourism 2020).

In the previously mentioned 10xCopenhagen strategy, part of the evidence base includes a substantial and ongoing focus on Copenhageners' perception and experience of tourism in their daily lives. The strategy's supporting research included surveys of more than 2,000 locals as well as nine focus group interviews and workshops with local residents and businesses in different neighborhoods, urban planners, tourism professionals, and eight expert interviews (10xCopenhagen 2020). The Resident Sentiment Index is a quantitative analysis of local sentiment toward tourism, including the potential problems caused by tourism as well as the locals' readiness for an increased number of visitors in the future. A recent opinion piece in Politiken by the Board of Wonderful Copenhagen highlighted that one of the critical success factors for Copenhagen's tourism industry is that any tourism-related developments are supported by local residents and indeed to proactively avoid overtourism and the antitourism movements seen in cities such as Barcelona and Venice (Wonderful Copenhagen Board 2020). According to the Board this requires a combination of measures ranging from urban planning to traffic regulation and better dispersal of visitors throughout the capital region and the year. The Board considers that this may be achieved through effective marketing and promotion targeting specific segments.

The coronavirus pandemic has meant that many local communities and residents now have a keener appreciation of the importance of tourism at the local destination level as well as the economic dependency on the previously successful sector. The devastation of tourism dependent economies, which tends to coincide with the very destinations that previously suffered from overtourism, meant that many local communities affected by the coronavirus pandemic lost their livelihoods almost overnight. In Venice, which received an estimated 26 million visitors in 2019, tourism gradually resumed from June 2020, but with no non-European tourists who usually make up around half of all visitors as well as a total absence of cruise ships. This means that the tourism economy, which previously employed around 65 percent of the population is still nowhere near recovering in the short term (Conradi 2020). A similar picture presents itself in London where at the beginning of 2021 the main tourist areas remained virtually empty with shops, restaurants, and hotels closed due to lack of demand.

The coronavirus pandemic provided an opportune time to take action to reshape the future of tourism in destinations around the world in order to prevent overtourism from returning or occurring in the first place. The aim of tourism should always be for local communities to be the main beneficiaries and thrive as a result of tourism development, rather than suffer as a consequence of poorly planned tourism based on a volume-driven business model. Ultimately, tourism is a force for good, but in recent years this has been overshadowed by the emergence of the overtourism phenomenon. As a consequence of the coronavirus pandemic, travel and tourism came to a virtual standstill for the first time in over 50 years and this provided an opportunity for destinations and their communities to consider how they would like tourism to restart and recover. However, community-centric recovery will not happen accidentally nor overnight—it will require a concerted and deliberate effort according to the Travel Foundation for destinations to come back better and stronger.

This means that destinations will need to carefully assess which visitor segments bring the most benefit to the local community from an economic, social, and environmental perspective. These visitor segments will then need to be targeted in order to optimize the potential benefits from tourism at the destination level. Now is a good time to be challenging the previous modus operandi and ask questions as to what a better tourism future might look like to ensure that destinations first and foremost serve local people's needs. An example of this is the Seychelles that has taken the drastic action not to welcome cruise ships until 2022. This reflects the fact that cruise ships have been a major "spreader" of the coronavirus and the ban is an attempt to mitigate the impact of the coronavirus pandemic on the island.

Edinburgh City Council in Scotland, UK, set up an action group comprising tourism leaders and council representatives to consider how the city's tourism industry would best recover from the coronavirus pandemic without reverting to overtourism (Edinburgh launches new initiative to support the hard-hit tourism and hospitality sector—The City of Edinburgh Council 2020). The city is seeking to put its people, place, and environment at the heart of its plans and remains committed to prioritizing sustainable and responsible tourism once tourism restarts.

Action needs to be taken at the destination level to help plan better for future growth and maintain a positive image of the tourism sector in the long term. European cities like Barcelona and countries such as Iceland and New Zealand have established new planning systems to finance infrastructure and protect major cultural heritage attractions as well as the wellbeing of their local population.

## Key Takeaways

- DMOs must actively seek to engage with the local host population and community to ensure that tourism delivers maximum benefits at the local destination level while at the same time minimizing any negative social and environmental impacts.

- An increasing number of destinations and DMOs including Amsterdam, Barcelona, and Copenhagen are actively engaging with representatives of the local community and residents in order to monitor overtourism and understand tourism's impact on the residents' quality of life as well as any negative perceptions.
- People and planet are increasingly placed ahead of profit, for example, through the development of social enterprise models for tourism operations.

# CHAPTER 9

# Funding Effective Destination Management and Infrastructure

## Introduction

This chapter considers how DMOs need to move away from being purely promotional bodies toward managing and coordinating destinations effectively. The challenge for many regional and local destinations remains how to fund the required investment in tourism-related infrastructure and services to help better manage visitor flows and mitigate overtourism.

The use of public space is free for all including visitors, but the maintenance and repair costs are funded by local taxpayers highlighting some of the invisible costs caused by increased tourist flows. The implication for DMOs is a shift away from marketing and promotion toward managing wider destination issues as highlighted previously.

Although, many destinations are keen to become more sustainable and avoid overtourism this requires a commitment to implementing sustainable development principles to deliver the desired goals and outcomes. The idea of imposing taxes and/or levies on international visitors is not new, but it remains highly controversial in many destinations and is often met with skepticism especially from private sector stakeholders and industry players.

## Making Destination Management Sustainable Long Term

Many destinations impose a relatively small city or environmental tax on tourists staying in registered accommodation establishments, which means those staying in privately rented accommodation such as Airbnb and day visitors do not have to pay the tax. This is the case in Amsterdam where overnight guests are charged a flat rate of €3 per night and a further 7 percent is added to your room bill when staying in registered accommodation (Tourist tax (toeristenbelasting) 2021). This approach is somewhat counterproductive as it targets those visitors who tend to spend the most in the destination while at the same time being less likely to cause negative impacts. On the other hand, daytrippers who frequently arrive in large groups causing congestion and typically spending very little in the destination are not taxed. This is likely due to the fact that it can be difficult to capture day visitors, especially if they are not part of a group. Thus, from an administrative point of view it is easier to just charge those staying in registered overnight accommodation.

## Tourist Taxes and Fees

Venice, which until March 2020 was one of the most overcrowded destinations in the world, was due to introduce a tax on daytrippers in July 2020 in an attempt to control visitor numbers (Dunford 2020). However, the tax was postponed until 2021 due to the coronavirus pandemic. The proposed tax is part of Venice's drive to rethink its tourism system and transition toward a model based on quality and sustainability at its core. According to Paola Mar, the city's councillor for tourism: "the goal is to trigger a renaissance of the city…. We want to attract visitors for longer stays and encourage a 'slower' type of tourism. Things cannot go back to how they were" (Dunford 2020).

Bhutan is perhaps the most well-known niche destination to have imposed a high tax (or more accurately an entry fee that requires a minimum expenditure per day) for visitors as well as limiting the number of foreign tourists visiting the country at any given time. This high-value, low-impact tourism model was introduced in line with the country's gross national happiness development model, which argues that an economy is not an economy if it does not promote sustainability, community wellbeing, and social harmony. The Bhutanese tourism policy aims to protect and share the country's natural beauty while preserving the local cultural traditions and way of life while benefiting from the jobs and foreign income generated by tourists. The daily charge of USD250 per day includes a USD65 sustainable development fee and a USD40 visa charge. Until recently regional visitors from India, Bangladesh, and the Maldives were excluded from paying the daily charge. (Minimum Daily Package | Tourism Council of Bhutan 2021). However, these regional visitors now also have to spend a minimum per day. USD65 out of the USD250 fee goes toward funding free healthcare and education for all citizens, nonetheless, about a third of the population still lives in poverty. The Bhutanese population are thought to be proud of their tourism policy and the benefits that it brings to their country. Thus, this would appear to be a positive model to adopt for developing countries and emerging economies seeking to alleviate poverty through tourism development.

According to the OECD, in the case of Iceland, the National Infrastructure Plan and the Tourist Site Protection Fund were established to support and invest in natural and cultural sites that face pressure from tourism. Investment in both public and private tourism-related infrastructure funded by the scheme equated to ISK1.2 billion in 2019 (OECD Tourism Trends and Policies 2020 | en | OECD 2020). The plan and fund were launched in response to the key challenge facing the Icelandic tourism sector, which is how to maximize the economic contribution from the sector while protecting the assets that it depends on. The rapid growth in tourism has increased pressure on nature, infrastructure, and society. This means that tourism planning, infrastructure investment, data collection, tourist safety, and visitor flow management remain key priorities in Iceland. Furthermore, a new long-term Tourism Policy Framework for 2020 to 2030 with a strong emphasis on sustainability was published in 2019. It is supported by a new Tourism Impact Assessment Model, which takes the carrying capacity of the environment, infrastructure, society, and economy into account and is considered fundamental to the future development of Icelandic tourism (OECD Tourism Trends and Policies 2020 | en | OECD 2020).

Recent growth in the number of visitors to New Zealand has not only increased the benefits of tourism, but it has also highlighted that the benefits versus costs need to be considered carefully as they do not always fall in the same place. Growth in tourism has led to overcrowding in places causing increasing pressure on infrastructure as well as some of New Zealand's main natural attractions (OECD Tourism Trends and Policies

2020 | en | OECD 2020). The current funding model for visitor-related infrastructure was no longer considered to be fit for purpose and this was compounded by the absence of a direct relationship between visitor numbers and revenues. It is often difficult to derive an adequate revenue stream from natural attractions and related facilities such as visitor centers and toilets with the cost of upkeep falling on central or local government. In the case of local government, this can put particular pressure on budgets and be unaffordable, especially in less densely populated areas. In such cases, central government intervention is necessary to ensure that funding for conservation, tourism infrastructure, and services is on a financially stable footing, with those who benefit from the infrastructure and services provided contributing meaningfully toward the costs. With this in mind, New Zealand recently introduced a NZD35 International Visitor Conservation and Tourism Levy to secure the necessary resources to mitigate the impact of tourism at the local destination level. The levy is forecast to provide NZD450 million over five years and is earmarked for investment in tourism infrastructure and conservation in equal measures in accordance with an investment plan. At the same time, the private sector in New Zealand has launched an industry-led Tourism Sustainability Commitment Initiative.

In 2016, the Rwandan government doubled the fee to USD1,500 for tourists to visit the Gorillas, which resulted in an increase in revenues from USD15 million to USD19 million and a drop in visitors to the Volcanoes National Park from 22,000 to 15,000 per annum (Bellaigue 2020). However, the coronavirus pandemic has exposed the downside to this particular low-volume high-yield model as there are currently no wealthy foreigners visiting the National park and they are unlikely to return for some time. Thus, the Rwandan government is having to rethink its conservation strategy owing to the lack of revenues coming from the high visitor fees. In an attempt to encourage domestic and regional tourism during the coronavirus pandemic the entry fee to the Volcanoes National Park has been reduced in the hope that it will help preserve more local livelihoods.

In Japan, the introduction of the International Passenger Tax is to become a permanent source of funding for tourism promotion as well as being put toward innovative and cost-effective measures to develop the tourism offer and support tourism businesses. Measures include

enhancing immigration procedures, developing world-class tourist facilities, and creating new tourism content using regional resources (OECD
Tourism Trends and Policies 2020 | en | OECD 2020).

## Key Takeaways

- Any tourism taxes and levies introduced to fund and manage
  tourism-related infrastructure at the destination level needs to
  be fair and transparent. In turn they can be used to promote
  sustainable tourism including social inclusion, cultural-heritage, and environmental conservation.
- In the interest of fairness, fees charged should apply to all
  types of international visitors including overnight tourists and
  daytrippers. Fees can be varied by season in order to attract
  fewer or more visitors depending on the seasonality pattern.
- Any taxes or fees imposed need to be supported by a long-
  term investment plan prioritizing tourist-related infrastructure, natural and cultural-heritage conservation, and tourism
  product development.
- Any taxes and levies are typically collected nationally, but ideally should be distributed locally to encourage visitor dispersal
  and de-seasonalization.

# CHAPTER 10

# Maximizing the Benefits of Tourism at the Local Destination Level

## Introduction

Throughout this book the key factors affecting overtourism have been explored as well as how it may be prevented from reoccurring in the future through effective destination management. This means that the tourism sector should be managed and developed with the aim of maximizing the benefits at the local destination level on a sustainable basis considering people, planet, and profit.

Post the coronavirus pandemic it will be crucial for destinations and DMOs to embrace a positive approach to supporting the travel and tourism industry in order to recover and rebuild a stronger sector going forward that can act as a catalyst for improved sustainability and economic prosperity for local people.

## People, Planet, and Profit

Traditionally, DMOs have tended to focus on marketing and promoting tourism in close collaboration and partnership with both public and private sector stakeholders in order to maximize visitor numbers and tourism revenues. However, less effort has been dedicated to managing and mitigating any negative social and environmental impacts arising due to rapid growth in visitor numbers. Failure to address the negative impacts of tourism inevitably leads to an eventual decline in tourism revenue. As visitor numbers continue to grow, public spaces, infrastructure, and the environment begin to struggle to cope and start suffering from the invisible burden of tourism, which in turn causes the visitor experience to deteriorate.

Overcoming overtourism requires a coordinated and joined-up effort among key stakeholders, be they private or public sector at national, regional, and local levels as well as engagement with the local host population and community. Better collaboration between public and private stakeholders will be crucial in terms of ensuring a safe and sustainable recovery of the tourism sector across the world.

Figure 10.1 illustrates the complexity and highly fragmented nature of the tourism industry and its public and private sector stakeholders as well as the local host community and population. For several years there has been a tendency to confuse sustainability with "green" by focusing exclusively on the environmental aspects of sustainability and not considering the social aspects. In order to tackle overtourism, destinations must adopt a holistic approach that considers all three pillars of sustainability: economic, environmental, and social to maximize the local benefits of the tourism sector while remaining competitive. The rise in overtourism followed by no tourism as a consequence of the coronavirus pandemic have highlighted the need for all three pillars of sustainability to be taken into account in order to manage a destination effectively and achieve a balance in the long term.

**Social:** Islands and smaller destinations typically have small populations to serve growing numbers of visitors, hence the need to focus on low-impact high-yield tourism—ideally those who want to engage with the destination in terms of its local people and culture without causing conflict. There is a limit to the number of people a small host population can serve and this needs to be taken into consideration when planning for the future. Larger destinations and cities can usually cope with larger volumes of visitors as their infrastructure is designed to accommodate larger volumes. However, large volumes of daytrippers arriving, by cruise ship or coach, at the same time can cause congestion and need to be carefully managed.

**Environment:** A diverse and stunning natural environment is often the main destination attractor for the majority of visitors especially in rural and coastal areas. However, sustainable tourism is obviously about

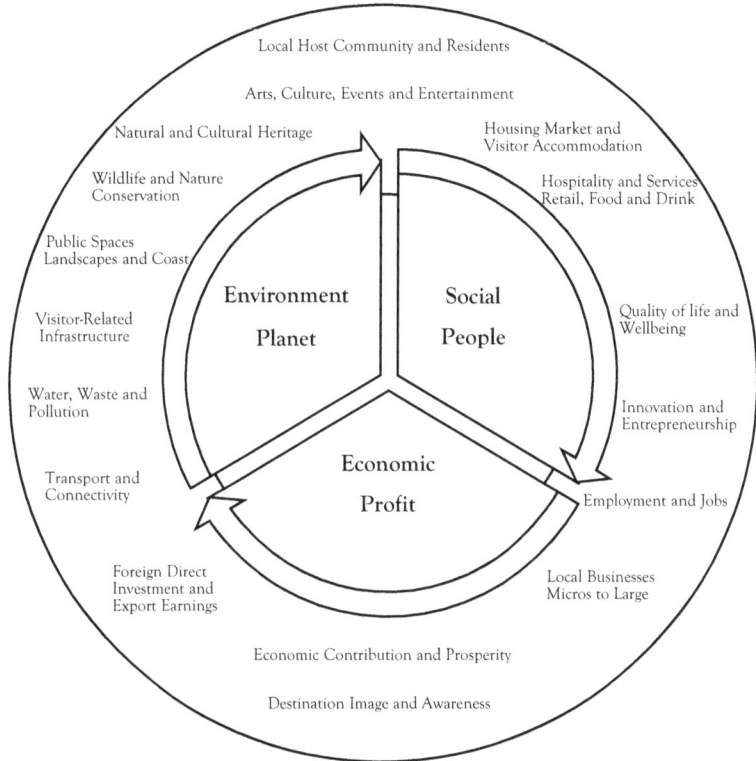

*Figure 10.1 Sustainable tourism model*

much more than visitors enjoying an attractive and pristine natural environment. It is about stewardship and preservation to maintain or even enhance the environment. It is crucially, also, about minimizing the impact as well as good management of visitor flows to avoid congestion and overcrowding leading to overtourism and potentially causing environmental degradation.

Tourists search for an authentic experience, but frequently do not get it owing to a combination of globalization, mass marketing, global tourism giants, consumer buying patterns, and congestion. This has created a sort of homogenous tourism product that could be replicated anywhere in the world. It is in some mainstream global operators' interest as when one destination faces a crisis or challenge then another is ready to take its place and nobody can really tell the difference, this is especially true of mass tourism resort destinations. Thus, destinations need to invest strategically in their product offering, differentiation, and quality of experience as returning visitors and experienced travelers are always searching for new authentic and distinct experiences and places to visit.

**Economic:** Many destinations have the opportunity to enhance the economic contribution of the tourism sector by focusing on niche low-impact high-yield visitors. Rather than think about visitors purely in terms of volume there is a need to focus on those visitors who offer the greatest potential in terms of visitor spends, stay overnight, and who are willing to visit outside the peak season. That is, those who deliver the greatest benefits locally be they economic, social, or environmental.

A good example of a destination that has placed sustainability at the heart of its tourism industry is Fogo Island in Newfoundland, Canada. Fogo Island is the largest of the offshore islands of Newfoundland and Labrador. The island is about 25km long and 14km wide covering a total area of 237m$^2$ with a population of 2,244 in 2016 (Fogo Island (Newfoundland and Labrador) 2021). The island attracts a wide range of visitors interested in its history, local wildlife, and other attractions such as drifting icebergs and whales. It has a number of popular walking trails as well as a range of local museums and historic houses. Fogo Island Arts provides a platform for contemporary arts and crafts on the island via a series of residencies hosted at different architecturally striking studios around the island.

Fogo Island is connected to mainland Newfoundland by a daily ferry service and also has a small airfield capable of servicing small charter or private jets, but there are no regular scheduled commercial flights to the island. This is important as it means that the journey to Fogo Island is a major part of the experience for most visitors. At the same time, it limits the number of visitors coming to the island so that it does not become overcrowded by visitors overwhelming the local population.

Central to the development of Fogo Island's high-yield low-volume approach to tourism was the opening of Fogo Island Inn in 2013, which has been instrumental in facilitating the continuing process of cultural and economic revitalization on Fogo Island. Newfoundland's remote communities, including Fogo Island, offer specific and pure forms of hospitality and social richness (as documented in Annie Proulx's Pullitzer

Prize-winning novel: The Shipping News). The development of Fogo Island Inn was an opportunity to use a social business model and design as a means to fortifying culture and place, while at the same time giving Fogo Island relevance in a contemporary world and enhancing the economic prospects for the community. In addition to acting as a catalyst to revive traditional building techniques, the Inn and its associated projects have created substantial employment opportunities (153 jobs in 2017) in a region previously devastated by the decline in the traditional cod fishing, and Fogo Islanders have acquired new skills to sustain themselves for years to come. Unique to Fogo Island Inn is the Community Host Programme that matches a person from the local community with guests to the Inn to help them orientate and experience the island. The community hosts are passionate, lifelong Fogo Islanders who are pleased to offer their insights into the island's natural and cultural heritage.

Critical to the success of Fogo and the Fogo Island Inn is the innovative social business model followed. The Inn is a community-owned asset where 100 percent of operating surpluses are reinvested in the community of Fogo Island. As such, the Inn is promoting sustainable economic prosperity for a community that stood on the brink of distinction in the not too distant past.

The multi award-winning Fogo Island Inn was built using primarily private philanthropic funds with the addition of some government grants, and there are no financial contributors seeking a return on their investment. The success of the Inn benefits no individuals, but rather the island's community at large and is an investment in a different way of thinking. As may be seen from the following diagram, money spent at Fogo Island Inn directly contributes to the wellbeing of one of Canada's oldest European settled communities. According to Shorefast, the commercial Fogo Island Inn strives to achieve social goals—this "not-just-for-profit" approach to business is considered a model for a more positive and productive relationship between capital and community. Shorefast, a registered Canadian charity with the mandate to help secure a resilient future for Fogo Island, developed the Economic Nutrition model by way of its social businesses, Fogo Island Inn and the Woodshop on Fogo Island (see Figure 10.2).

Fogo Island is a good example of how community-focused tourism can be used as a tool to revitalize a small and remote community through

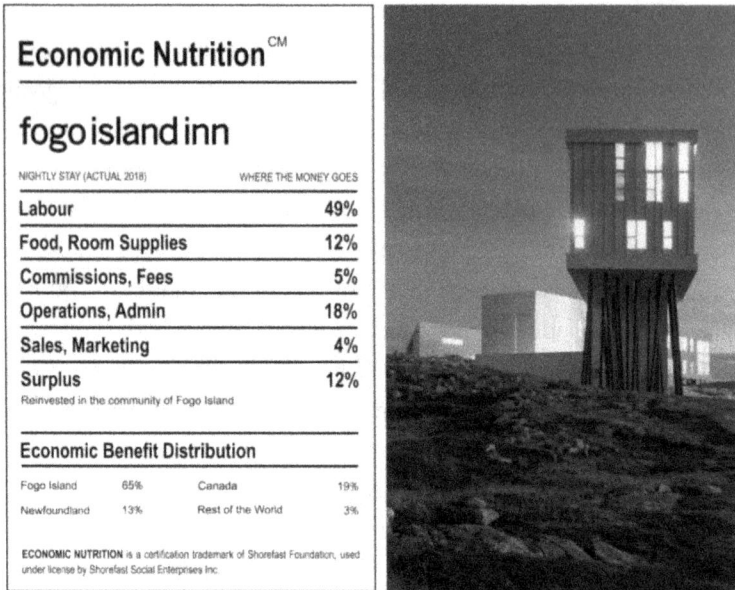

**Economic Nutrition**<sup>CM</sup>

**fogo island inn**

| NIGHTLY STAY (ACTUAL 2018) | WHERE THE MONEY GOES |
|---|---|
| Labour | 49% |
| Food, Room Supplies | 12% |
| Commissions, Fees | 5% |
| Operations, Admin | 18% |
| Sales, Marketing | 4% |
| Surplus<br>Reinvested in the community of Fogo Island | 12% |

**Economic Benefit Distribution**

| Fogo Island | 65% | Canada | 19% |
|---|---|---|---|
| Newfoundland | 13% | Rest of the World | 3% |

ECONOMIC NUTRITION is a certification trademark of Shorefast Foundation, used under license by Shorefast Social Enterprises Inc.

*Figure 10.2  Fogo Island Inn economic nutrition model*

Source: Fogo Island Inn and Shorefast

stakeholder engagement and passionate leadership. The social enterprise model is one that can be applied in many situations. However, critical to the long-term success is that such enterprises are managed and operated in a professional manner delivering a high-quality product and service.

## Policy Responses to Overtourism

According to the OECD, a number of destinations have introduced policy measures to address the issue of overtourism and overcrowding at popular destinations. These include spreading the economic and other benefits to areas that attract fewer visitors by developing new products to minimize the impacts of seasonality as well as encouraging increased productivity, better resource utilization, and more stable employment (OECD Tourism Trends and Policies 2020 | en | OECD 2020). It suggests that tourism can no longer simply be measured in terms of arrivals, jobs, and income. Ensuring that local communities can more equally benefit from tourism has become a prevailing policy trend among governments and some progress has been made. This includes developing coherent, forward-looking approaches to the design of tourism policies and programs, supported by long-term strategies and flexible action plans. Furthermore, there is a need to strengthen coordination mechanisms and delivery structures to ensure that policies agreed at national level are consistently delivered at the regional and local levels. For such policies to be successful requires engagement with communities and businesses to ensure local destinations can fully share the benefits of a dynamic tourism economy.

The OECD recommends that destinations help prepare tourism businesses for a digital future as well as rethinking tourism success for sustainable growth. This means placing more focus on the environmental and sociocultural pillars of sustainability as well as ensuring efforts to grow tourism are pursued within the wider context of city, local, regional, and national strategies in close collaboration with local public and private sector stakeholders (OECD Tourism Trends and Policies 2020 | en | OECD 2020). Kate Raworth's Doughnut economy approach aims to thrive rather than letting growth be a goal in itself, which is something the tourism industry could learn from. Amsterdam has adopted this approach and is using the coronavirus pandemic as a catalyst to introduce a more sustainable and responsible tourism model. The aim is to attract the right kind of visitor, rather than continuously striving for an increasing number of visitors, in order to ensure that tourism does not harm the "livability" of the city and that it has a balanced economy.

The EU recognizes that tourism matters and that it is time to act on key policy priorities to ensure that tourism in Europe continues to be a key driver of economic growth and job creation, fostering European values and citizenship (European Parliament 2018). This is recognized by the Treaty of Lisbon, which gives the EU the responsibility to promote the competitiveness of the European tourism sector by creating a favorable environment for its growth and development and by establishing an integrated approach to the travel and tourism sector. It goes on to state that in order to formulate effective tourism policies, a holistic European approach is needed considering the multiple impacts of the sector as well as the wide spectrum of stakeholders affected by tourism (The Treaty of Lisbon | Fact Sheets on the European Union | European Parliament 2009). The European Tourism Manifesto identifies that it is crucial to support good practice in capacity and destination management so that supply adapts successfully to demand, and to ensure that the quality of the visitor experience goes hand in hand with the quality of life of local host communities (European Parliament 2018).

Responsible Tourism's vision to avoid future overtourism involves a tourism footprint that is more dispersed, and less focused on a few global hotspots. Destinations that will manage tourism first and foremost to protect local people's quality of life and their natural and cultural heritage. In some ways, the coronavirus pandemic may help to achieve this sooner as it is thought that people are more likely to travel less, but for longer to more remote destinations once international travel starts to recover. However, many people and destinations will be financially constrained, which is likely to result in lower prices and less commitment to sustainability at least in the short term.

It is clear that destinations need to consider how appropriate local and regional development strategies can encourage the dispersal of tourists away from the most popular areas and help to reduce seasonality. Such strategies typically require stimulating innovative product and infrastructure development outside tourism hotspots to relieve pressure points and attract new types of visitors (ideally higher spending overnight visitors) who are able to visit outside the peak season.

# Key Takeaways

- Overtourism is a complex multidimensional issue that requires effective destinations management solutions in order to ensure that tourism delivers maximum local benefits while minimizing any negative social, environmental, and economic impacts.
- Destinations and DMOs need short-, medium- and long-term strategies to manage tourism growth and avoid overtourism as well as forming an integral part of the wider destination economy and planning.
- In order to achieve long-term sustainable success destinations and DMOs must engage effectively with key industry stakeholders, the local community, and residents as well as visitors.

# Bibliography

AECO. 2020. "AECO | Association Of Arctic Expedition Cruise Operators." [online] Available at https://aeco.no/ (accessed December 15, 2020).

Airbnb Newsroom. 2017. "Airbnb Partners With Visit Denmark." [online] Available at https://news.airbnb.com/airbnb-partners-with-visitdenmark/ (accessed January 4, 2021).

Ajuntament.barcelona.cat. 2020. "Barcelona Tourism For 2020—A Collective Strategy For Sustainable Tourism." [online] Available at https://ajuntament. barcelona.cat/ turisme/sites/default/files/barcelona_tourism_for_2020.pdf (accessed January 5, 2021).

Arlidge, J. 2020. *Inn Trouble*. Sunday Times Magazine.

Avoid Crowds. 2020. "Analyzing Barcelona's Cruise Traffic—Avoid Crowds." [online] Available at https://avoid-crowds.com/analyzing-barcelona-cruise-traffic/ (accessed January 7, 2021).

BBC News. 2020. "Birling Gap: Warning After Visitors Pictured Walking Near Cliff Edges." [online] Available at https://bbc.co.uk/news/uk-england-sussex-52796601 (Accessed December 15, 2020).

Bellaigue, C. 2020. "The End Of Tourism? [online]" *The Guardian*. Available at https://theguardian.com/travel/2020/jun/18/end-of-tourism-coronavirus-pandemic-travel-industry (accessed January 5, 2021).

Brady, S. 2019. "Is Copenhagen the Latest City to Fall Victim to Overtourism?." *Lonely Planet*, available at https://lonelyplanet.com/articles/copenhagen-overtourism?utm_source=twitter&utm_medium=social&utm_campaign=article (accessed December 14, 2020).

Bremner, C. 2019. "Megatrends Shaping The Future Of Travel: 2019 Edition." [online] www.euromonitor.com. available at https://go.euromonitor.com/WTM19.html (accessed January 7, 2021).

Burgen, S. 2019. "Barcelona Mayor Promises Crackdown On Cruise Ships." [online] *The Guardian*. Available at https://theguardian.com/cities/2019/jul/05/barcelona-mayor-promises-crackdown-cruise-ships (accessed January 4, 2021).

Butler, R. 1980. *The Concept of A Tourism Area Cycle of Evolution: Implications For Management Resources*. Canadian Geographer, Wiley Online Library.

Calderwood, L., and M. Soshkin. 2019. "The Travel & Tourism Competitiveness Report 2019." [online] *World Economic Forum*. Available at https://weforum.org/reports/the-travel-tourism-competitiveness-report-2019 (accessed January 7, 2021).

Connolly, K., and S. Smith. 2019. "A Rising Tide: 'Overtourism' and the Curse of the Cruise Ships." [online] www.theguardian.com. Available at https://theguardian.com/business/2019/sep/16/a-rising-tide-overtourism-and-the-curse-of-the-cruise-ships (accessed December 15, 2020).

Conradi, P. 2020. "No Cruise Is Good News For Tourists In Empty Venice." [online] *Thetimes.co.uk*. Available at https://thetimes.co.uk/article/no-cruise-is-good-news-for-tourists-in-empty-venice-qrpl3r577 (accessed December 15, 2020).

Crasta, R. 2019. "Overtourism: Tourism, Travel and Rights: Perspectives and Solutions. Cruising.org. 2020." *2019 Cruise Trends & Industry Outlook*. [online] Available at https://cruising.org/news-and-research/-/media/CLIA/Research/CLIA-2019-State-of-the-Industry.pdf (accessed January 7, 2021).

Dodds, R., and R. Butler. 2019. "The Phenomena of Overtourism: A Review | International Journal of Tourism Cities." [Online] *Emerald.com*. Available at https://emerald.com/insight/content/doi/10.1108/IJTC-06-2019-0090/full/html (accessed January 7, 2021).

Dodds, R., and R. Butler. 2019. "Overtourism: 1." [online] www.degruyter.com. Available at https://degruyter.com/overtourism (accessed January 6, 2021).

Dunford, J. 2020. "'Things Have To Change': Tourism Businesses Look to a Greener Future." [online] www.theguardian.com. Available at https://theguardian.com/travel/2020/may/28/things-had-to-change-tourism-businesses-look-to-a-greener-future (accessed January 5, 2021).

Ehotelier Insights. 2020. "Tourism Satisfaction: Importance, Measurability And Impacts—Insights." [online] Available at https://insights.ehotelier.com/insights/2020/04/30/tourism-satisfaction-importance-measurability-andimpacts/ (accessed January 4, 2021).

En.wikipedia.org. 2021. "Fogo Island (Newfoundland And Labrador)." [online] Available at https://en.wikipedia.org/wiki/Fogo_Island_(Newfoundland_and_Labrador) (accessed January 5, 2021).

ETC Corporate. 2019. "Gastronomy And Urban Experiences Among The Top Drivers Of Europe'S Attractiveness." [online] Available at https://etc-corporate.org/news/gastronomy-and-urban-experiences-among-the-top-drivers-of-europes-attractiveness/ (accessed December 15, 2020).

Euromonitor.com. 2020. "Travel 2040: Sustainability And Digital Transformation As Recovery Drivers." [online] Available at https://go.euromonitor.com/webinar-travel-2020-travel-2040-digital-transformation.html (accessed January 7, 2021).

Euromonitor.com. 2020. "The Impact Of Coronavirus On The Global Economy | Market Research Report | Euromonitor." [online] Available at https://euromonitor.com/the-impact-of-coronavirus-on-the-global-economy/report (accessed January 7, 2021).

Europarl.europa.eu. 2009. "The Treaty Of Lisbon | Fact Sheets On The European Union | European Parliament." [online] Available at: https://europarl.europa. eu/factsheets/en/sheet/5/the-treaty-of-lisbon (accessed January 5, 2021).

Frances, J. 2020. "Responsible Tourism Manifesto For Change Chapter one: Aviation and the Climate Crisis." [online] responsibletravel.com. Available at https://responsibletravel.com/copy/manifesto-aviation (accessed December 15, 2020).

Fox, D. 2020. "The Coronavirus: How Pandemics of the Past Have Changed The World." [online] Thetimes.co.uk. Available at https://thetimes.co.uk/ article/the-coronavirus-how-pandemics-of-the-past-have-changed-the-world-gswzl6rhz (accessed January 6, 2021).

Froelich, P. 2020. "Why The Travel Industry Will Be Stronger And Better After Coronavirus." [online] www.nypost.com. Available at https://nypost. com/2020/03/29/why-the-travel-industry-will-be-stronger-and-better-after-coronavirus/ (accessed January 5, 2021).

Geerts, W. 2020. "WTM 2018: Megatrends Shaping The Future of Travel | Market Research Report | Euromonitor." [online] Euromonitor.com. Available at https://euromonitor.com/wtm-2018-megatrends-shaping-the-future-of-travel/report (accessed December 15, 2020).

Gentleman, A. 2020. "Everyone Is In That Fine Line Between Death And Life': Inside Everest's Deadliest Queue." [online] www.theguardian.com. Available at https://theguardian.com/world/2020/jun/06/everyone-is-in-that-fine-line-between-death-and-life-inside-everests-deadliest-queue (accessed January 5, 2021).

Gstcouncil.org. 2020. "GSTC Criteria | Global Sustainable Tourism Council (GSTC)." [online] Available at https://gstcouncil.org/gstc-criteria/ (accessed January 6, 2021).

Hawkins, R., and V. Middleton. 1998. "Sustainable Tourism 1st Edition." [online] www.routledge.com. Available at https://routledge.com/Sustainable-Tourism/ Hawkins-Middleton/p/book/9780750623858 (accessed January 6, 2021).

Hindle, D. 2020. "Now's The Time to Start Planning for Business Recovery." [online] Travelmole.com. Available at https://travelmole.com/news_feature. php? news_id=2041875 (accessed January 5, 2021).

Hunter, M. 2020. "What Will Travel Look Like After Coronavirus?" [online] www. cnn.com. Available at https://edition.cnn.com/travel/article/coronavirus-travel-industry-changes/index.html (accessed January 5, 2021).

Husted, P. 2020. "Alt For Mange Turister: Lonely Planet Advarer Mod At Besøge København." [online] Politiken. Available at https://politiken.dk/rejser/ art7378392/Lonely-Planet-advarer-mod-at-besøge-København (accessed December14, 2020).

IATA. 2021. "IATA History—Growth And Development." [online] Available at https://iata.org/en/about/history/history-growth-and-development/ (accessed January 7, 2021).

ICAO. 2021. "Effects of Novel Coronavirus (COVID-19) On Civil Aviation: Economic Impact Analysis." [online] Available at https://icao.int/sustainability/Documents/COVID-19/ICAO_Coronavirus_Econ_Impact.pdf (accessed January 22, 2021).

Islandsstofa.is. 2012. "Long-Term Strategy For The Iceland Tourism Industry." [online] Available at https://islandsstofa.is/media/1/final-long-term-strategy-for-icelandic-tourism-industry-270213kh.pdf (accessed January 4, 2021).

Jeffrey, F. 2020. "A Response To 'The End Of Tourism?'." [online] www.travelweekly.co.uk. Available at https://travelweekly.co.uk/articles/376836/comment-a-response-to-the-end-of-tourism (accessed January 5, 2021).

Jennings, R. 2019. "Boracay Beach Inspires New, Foreign-Invested Tourism Zones In The Philippines." [online] *Forbes*. Available at https://forbes.com/sites/ralphjennings/2019/10/31/boracay-beach-inspires-new-foreign-invested-tourism-zones-in-the-philippines/?sh=6df7b76a8551 (accessed January 4, 2021).

Keating, D. 2020. "EU Unveils Plan to Reopen Tourism This Summer." [online] www.forbes.com. Available at https://forbes.com/sites/davekeating/2020/05/13/eu-unveils-plan-to-reopen-tourism-this-summer/ (accessed January 5, 2021).

Krippendorf, J., and V. Andrassy. 1984. *The Holiday Makers: Understanding the Impact of Leisure and Travel*. Oxford: Butterworth-Heinemann.

Kusmer, A. 2020. "Amsterdam'S Coronavirus Recovery Plan Embraces 'Doughnut Economics' For People and the Planet." [online] www.pri.org. Available at https://pri.org/stories/2020-05-11/amsterdam-s-coronavirus-recovery-plan-embraces-doughnut-economics-people-and (accessed January 5, 2021).

Lansky, D. 2020. [online] Douglansky.com. Available at https://douglansky.com/about/ (accessed January 4, 2021).

Lalor, A. 2020. "Amsterdam's Old City Centre Will Be Airbnb-Free From July 1—Dutchreview." [online] www.dutchreview.com. Available at https://dutchreview.com/news/dutch/amsterdams-city-centre-will-be-airbnb-free-from-july-1/ (accessed January 5, 2021).

Lilit Marcus, C. 2021. "Seychelles Bans Cruise Ships Through 2021 to Prevent Covid-19 Spread." [online] *CNN*. Available at https://cnn.com/travel/article/seychelles-cruise-ship-ban-coronavirus/index.html (accessed January 4, 2021).

Medina, F. 2020. "Opinion: After Coronavirus, Lisbon Is Turning Away From Airbnb And Using Holiday Rentals As Key Worker Homes." [online] www.independent.co.uk. Available at https://independent.co.uk/voices/coronavirus-lisbon-portugal-airbnb-homes-key-workers-a9601246.html?fbclid=IwAR32rSEgTPAjUNA4JQtFt-FQS3ztOLUV13X6Y9d2C5SbPRqlPJEQQtU6Cn4 (accessed January 5, 2021).

McKinsey & Company. 2017. "World Travel & Tourism Council (WTTC) | Travel & Tourism Representative Council." [online] Wttc.org. Available at https://wttc.org/ (accessed December 15, 2020).

Mbie.govt.nz. 2019. "New Zealand—Aotearoa Government Tourism Strategy." [online] Available at https://mbie.govt.nz/assets/8d33d0afb7/2019-new-zealand-aotearoa-government-tourism-strategy.pdf (accessed January 7, 2021).

Milano, C., Dr. 2017. *Overtourism and Tourism-Phobia—A Complex Journey Between Economic Gain and Socio-Cultural Preservation.* Seminar, University of Brighton.

Miljovernfondet.no. 2021. "About The Fund | Svalbards Miljøvernfond." [online] Available at https://miljovernfondet.no/en/about-svalbard-environmental-protection-fund/ (accessed January 7, 2021).

Neate, R., and S. Bowers. 2012. "Costa Concordia: £300M Wiped Off Ship Owner's Fortune." [online] www.theguardian.com. Available at https://theguardian.com/world/2012/jan/16/costa-concordia-ship-owner-fortune (accessed January 7, 2021).

OECD. 2020. "OECD Tourism Trends And Policies 2020 | En | OECD." [online] Available at http://oecd.org/cfe/tourism/oecd-tourism-trends-and-policies-20767773.htm (accessed January 5, 2021).

Openknowledge.worldbank.org. 2020. "Rebuilding Tourism Competitiveness—Tourism Response, Recovery And Resilience To The Covid-19 Crisis." [online] Available at https://openknowledge.worldbank.org/bitstream/handle/10986/34348/Rebuilding-Tourism-Competitiveness-Tourism-response-recovery-and-resilience-to-the-COVID-19-crisis.pdf?sequence=5&isAllowed=y (accessed January 5, 2021).

Pallis, T. 2015. "Cruise Shipping and Urban Development: State of the Art of the Industry and Cruise Ports." *International Transport Forum Discussion Papers*, No. 2015/14, OECD Publishing, Paris, https://doi.org/10.1787/5jrvzrlw74nv-en

Pechlaner, H., E, Innerhofer, and G. Erschbamer. 2020. *Overtourism: Tourism Management And Solutions.* Abingdon, Oxon: Routledge.

Peeters, P. et al. 2018. "Research for TRAN Committee—Overtourism: impact and possible policy response, Policy Department for Structural and Cohesion Policies, EU Directorate-General for Internal Policies." [online] Available at https://europarl.europa.eu/RegData/etudes/STUD/2018/629184/IPOL_STU(2018)629184_EN.pdf (accessed January 7, 2021).

Roberts, H. 2020. "Venice to Give Cruise Ships a Wide Berth." [online] Ft.com. Available at https://ft.com/content/6e21302e-b922-11e9-96bd-8e884d3ea203 (accessed December 15, 2020).

Rodrigue, J., 2019. "Section About Air Transport Completely Updated | The Geography Of Transport Systems." [online] *Transportgeography.org*. Available at https://transportgeography.org/?p=14012 (accessed January 7, 2021).

Sampson, J. 2020. "Communities Belong at the Center of Tourism—Travel Foundation." [online] *Travel Foundation*. Available at https://thetravelfoundation.org.uk/communities-center-recovery/ (accessed January 7, 2021).

Séraphin, H., and T. Gladkikh. 2020. *Overtourism: Causes, Implications and Solutions*. Palgrave.

Sheivachman, A. 2019. "The Rise and Fall Of Iceland's Tourism Miracle." [online] Skift. Available at https://skift.com/2019/09/11/the-rise-and-fall-of-icelands-tourism-miracle/ (accessed January 22, 2021).

Smith, E. 2021. "Evolution Of Cruising | A Brief History Of Cruise | Cruise118." [online] Keep up with the Latest Cruise News with Cruise118.com. Available at https://cruise118.com/news/the-evolution-of-cruising/ (accessed January 7, 2021).

Smith, J. 2020. "Does The COVID-19 Emergency Mean Over-Tourism Is Over? | WTM Global Hub." [online] www.hub.wtm.com. Available at https://hub.wtm.com/does-the-covid-19-emergency-mean-over-tourism-is-over/ (accessed January 5, 2021).

Statistics Iceland. 2021. "Statistics Iceland: Tourism." [online] Available at https://statice.is/statistics/business-sectors/tourism/ (accessed January 7, 2021).

St Helena local enterprise and investment. 2019. "Enterprise St Helena Offers Local Enterprise And Investment." [online] Available at http://investinsthelena.com/ (accessed January 7, 2021).

Temperton, J. 2021. "Is This The End Of Airbnb?" [online] WIRED UK. Available at https://wired.co.uk/article/airbnb-coronavirus-losses (accessed January 5, 2021).

Tourism4sdgs.org. 2020. UNWTO Webinar "Agenda 2030 And Sdgs In Times Of COVID-19: The Chance To True Recovery"—Tourism For Sdgs. [online] Available at http://tourism4sdgs.org/events/unwto-webinar-agenda-2030-and-sdgs-in-times-of-covid-19-the-chance-to-true-recovery/ (accessed January 6, 2021).

Tourism.gov.bt. 2021. "Minimum Daily Package | Tourism Council of Bhutan." [online] Available at https://tourism.gov.bt/about-us/minimum-daily-package (accessed January 5, 2021).

Tourism.gov.mm. 2021. "Myanmar Tourism Statistics 2019." [online] Available at https://tourism.gov.mm/wp-content/uploads/2020/05/Myanmar-Tourism-Statisitcs-2019-1.pdf (accessed January 4, 2021).

Tourtellot, J. 2020. "Corona-Crisis: A Destination Management Opportunity.—Destination Stewardship Center." [online] www.destinationcenter.org. Available at https://destinationcenter.org/2020/03/corona-crisis-a-destination-management-opportunity/ (accessed January 5, 2021).

Travel Foundation. 2019. "Destinations At Risk: The Invisible Burden Of Tourism—Travel Foundation." [online] Available at https://thetravelfoundation.org.uk/invisible-burden/ (accessed January 4, 2021).

Tsang, A. 2020. "How Asian Social Media Transformed A Quiet U.K. Walking Spot (Published 2018)." [online] Nytimes.com. Available at https://nytimes.com/2018/10/12/world/europe/seven-sisters-cliffs-tourism-pictures.html (accessed December 15, 2020).

Tourismmanifesto.eu. 2021. "European Tourism Manifesto." [online] Available at https://tourismmanifesto.eu/ (accessed January 7, 2021).

UNWTO. 2021. "Tourism Back To 1990 Levels As Arrivals Fall By More Than 70%." [online] Available at https://unwto.org/news/tourism-back-to-1990-levels-as-arrivals-fall-by-more-than-70 (accessed January 22, 2021).

UNWTO. 2021. "UNWTO Tourism Data Dashboard | UNWTO." [online] Available at https://unwto.org/unwto-tourism-dashboard (accessed January 6, 2021).

UNWTO. 2020. "TOURISM 4 Sdgs | UNWTO." [online] Available at https://unwto.org/tourism4sdgs (accessed December 15, 2020).

UNWTO. 2020. "UNWTO And WHO Agree To Further Cooperation In COVID-19 Response | UNWTO." [online] Available at https://unwto.org/unwto-and-who-agree-to-further-cooperation-in-covid-19-response (accessed January 7, 2021).

UNWTO. 2019. "Guidelines For Institutional Strengthening of Destination Management Organizations (Dmos)—Preparing Dmos For New Challenges." [online] Available at https://e-unwto.org/doi/book/10.18111/9789284420841 (accessed January 7, 2021).

UNWTO. 2018. "A Practical Guide To Tourism Destination Management | UNWTO." [online] Available at https://unwto.org/global/ publication/ practical-guide-tourism-destination-management (accessed January 4, 2021).

UNWTO. 2017. "Tourism And The Sustainable Development Goals—Journey To 2030 | UNWTO." [online] Available at https://unwto.org/global/ publication/tourism-and-sustainable-development-goals-journey-2030 (accessed January 7, 2021).

UNWTO. 2008. "International Recommendations For Tourism Statistics 2008." [online] Available at https://e-unwto.org/doi/book/10.18111/9789211615210 (accessed January 4, 2021).

UNWTO. 1983. "Risks Of Saturation Of Tourist Carrying Capacity Overload In Holiday Destinations (English Version) | World Tourism Organization." [online] Available at https://e-unwto.org/doi/book/10.18111/9789284407545 (accessed January 6, 2021).

Wikipedia. 2021. "Allure of the Seas." [online] Available at https://en.wikipedia.org/wiki/Allure_of_the_Seas (accessed January 7, 2021).

Wonderful Copenhagen. 2021. "The Sustainable Turnaround Port | Wonderful Copenhagen." [online] Available at https://wonderfulcopenhagen.com/ cruise/sustainable-turnaround-port (accessed January 7, 2021).

Wonderful Copenhagen Board. 2020. "Sådan tackler vi masseturismen i København" [online} Politiken. Available at https//e-pages.dk/Politiken/493337 (accessed August 28, 2020).

Wood, M., M. Milstein, and K. Ahamed-Broadhurst. 2020. "Destinations At Risk: The Invisible Burden Of Tourism—Travel Foundation." [online] *Travel Foundation.* Available at https://thetravelfoundation.org.uk/invisible-burden/ (accessed December 15, 2020).

WTTC.org. 2020. "Recovery Scenarios & Economic Impact From COVID-19 | World Travel & Tourism Council (WTTC)." [online] Available at https://wttc.org/Research/Economic-Impact/Recovery-Scenarios (accessed January 22, 2021).

WTTC. 2021. "How Can You Promote Sustainable Travel?" [online] Available at https://worldtraveltourismcouncil.medium.com/how-can-you-promote-sustainable-travel-c9a19de03b4e (accessed January 7, 2021).

WTTC. 2021. "Travel & Tourism Economic Impact | World Travel & Tourism Council (WTTC)." [online] Available at https://wttc.org/Research/Economic-Impact (accessed January 6, 2021).

WTTC. 2020. "ICC And World Travel & Tourism Council Issue COVID-19 Restart Guide For The Travel & Tourism Sector." [online] Available at https://wttc.org/News-Article/ICC-and-World-Travel-and-Tourism-Council-issue-COVID-19-restart-guide-for-the-Travel-and-Tourism-sector (accessed January 6, 2021).

www.amsterdam.nl. 2021. "Tourist Tax (Toeristenbelasting)." [online] Available at https://amsterdam.nl/en/municipal-taxes/tourist-tax-(toeristenbelasting)/ (accessed January 5, 2021).

www.edinburgh.gov.uk. 2020. "Edinburgh Launches New Initiative To Support The Hard-Hit Tourism And Hospitality Sector—The City Of Edinburgh Council." [online] Available at https://edinburgh.gov.uk/news/article/12941/edinburgh-launches-new-initiative-to-support-the-hard-hit-tourism-and-hospitality-sector (accessed January 5, 2021).

10xCopenhagen. 2020. "10Xcopenhagen—Rethinking Tourism In Copenhagen Towards 2030." [online] Available at https://10xcopenhagen.com/ (accessed January 7, 2021).

# About the Author

**Helene von Magius Møgelhøj** is an expert advisor and speaker on sustainable tourism, hospitality, and economic development. She has over 20 years of international experience gained across the private, public, and third sectors. Her extensive knowledge and skills cover a broad spectrum of key issues ranging from tourism strategy formulation to sustainable destination planning and from assessment of financial viability to enhancing destination competitiveness.

Helene's specialist areas of expertise include:

- Sustainable urban and coastal resort planning, economic development, and strategy, including sustainability certification and environmental auditing.
- Market research, analysis, benchmarking, and product development as well as organizational and operational reviews.
- Business planning, financial appraisal, evaluation, and operational reviews.
- Program and project management with the ability to work to budget and tight timescales throughout the lifecycle from conceptualization through to design and implementation.
- Proactive public and private sector stakeholder engagement, influencing, communication, and partnership development.
- Facilitation of business and knowledge transfer networks for the tourism, hospitality, and environmental sectors to stimulate business growth and innovation.

Previously, Helene worked as destination development manager for the South East England Development Agency (SEEDA), where she managed a comprehensive tourism development program for the Hastings and Bexhill area on the Sussex coast in England. She worked closely with the knowledge base developing the tourism-related curriculum with

University of Brighton as well as supervising a PhD student and dedicated tourism researcher with the aim of building the tourism evidence base.

Prior to that Helene was a senior consultant at PKF carrying out a wide range of tourism, hotel, and leisure assignments in destinations as far flung as South Africa and Oman as well as Europe and in the United Kingdom.

Helene is a fellow of the Tourism Society.

# Index

## OTHER TITLES IN THE TOURISM AND HOSPITALITY MANAGEMENT COLLECTION

Betsy Bender Stringam, New Mexico State University, Editor

- *Food and Beverage Management in the Luxury Hotel Industry* by Sylvain Boussard
- *Targeting the Mature Traveler* by Jacqueline Jeynes
- *Hospitality* by Chris Sheppardson
- *Food and Architecture* by Subhadip Majumder, and Sounak Majumder
- *A Time of Change in Hospitality Leadership* by Chris Sheppardson
- *Improving Convention Center Management Using Business Analytics and Key Performance Indicators, Volume II* by Myles T. McGrane
- *Improving Convention Center Management Using Business Analytics and Key Performance Indicators, Volume I* by Myles T. McGrane
- *A Profile of the Hospitality Industry, Second Edition* by Betsy Bender Stringam
- *Cultural and Heritage Tourism and Management* by Tammie J. Kaufman
- *Marine Tourism, Climate Change, and Resilience in the Caribbean, Volume II* by Kreg Ettenger, Samantha Hogenson, and Martha Honey
- *Marketing Essentials for Independent Lodging* by Pamela Lanier
- *Marine Tourism, Climate Change, and Resiliency in the Caribbean, Volume I* by Samantha Hogenson, and Martha Honey
- *Catering and Convention Service Survival Guide in Hotels and Casinos* by Lisa Lynn Backus, and Patti J. Shock,

## Announcing the Business Expert Press Digital Library

*Concise e-books business students need for classroom and research*

This book can also be purchased in an e-book collection by your library as

- a one-time purchase,
- that is owned forever,
- allows for simultaneous readers,
- has no restrictions on printing, and
- can be downloaded as PDFs from within the library community.

Our digital library collections are a great solution to beat the rising cost of textbooks. E-books can be loaded into their course management systems or onto students' e-book readers. The **Business Expert Press** digital libraries are very affordable, with no obligation to buy in future years. For more information, please visit **www.businessexpertpress.com/librarians**. To set up a trial in the United States, please email **sales@businessexpertpress.com**.

www.ingramcontent.com/pod-product-compliance
Lightning Source LLC
Chambersburg PA
CBHW061332220326
41599CB00026B/5152